Inward
Traveler

Inward Traveler:

51 Ways to Explore the World Mindfully

Francine Toder, Ph.D.

Aziri Books
Palo Alto, California

Also by Francine Toder

When Your Child is Gone: Learning to Live Again

Your Kids Are Grown: Moving on With and Without Them

The Vintage Years: Finding Your Inner Artist (Writer, Musician, Visual Artist) After Sixty

Aziri Books
380 Hamilton Avenue, #1735
Palo Alto, California 94302

Printed in the United States of America
First Edition, 2018

Library of Congress Control Number: 2018942554
Toder, Francine
Inward Traveler: 51 Ways to Explore the World Mindfully—1ˢᵗ ed.
Includes bibliographic references

ISBN-13: 978-0-9882059-4-9

Mind/Body (Mindfulness), Psychology, Travel, Memoir

Cover photo: Jeremy Vessey (Unsplash)
Couple Talking, illustration: Joseph Hustein
Kaleidoscope mandala: Karen Arnold
Yoga illustration, tai chi photo: courtesy of Pickapic/Freepik
Yoga pose photo: Jacob Postuma (Unsplash)
Waterway to Oslo photo: William Faucher (Unsplash)
Interior Photos: Francine Toder, Joseph Hustein

AziriBooks.com

Dedication

Inward Traveler is dedicated to my four grandchildren Jake, Wyatt, Wesley, and Skylar who live each day totally in the moment, with curiosity and wonder—taking in and playing with all they encounter. Being around them inspires, invigorates, and reminds me of our human potential to understand and appreciate our lives on a daily basis.

Table of Contents

Introduction   Page   1

Traditions and viewpoints   Page   7

  1.   Buddhist and Tao principles: novel ways to meditate
  2.   Yoga and Tai Chi: taking meditation on the road
  3.   Awe: seeing life with a beginner's mind
  4.   Wonder: where the oceans meet
  5.   Contemplative journeys: walking meditation—virtual and real
  6.   Heighten personal meaning through travel

Maximizing Travel: before, during & afterwards   Page   29

  7.   Enhance your experience *beforehand*: positive anticipation
  8.   Make your dream happen: expand the options
  9.   Transportation hassles: reframe your experience
  10. Trust your instinct, judgment, and experience
  11. Shut down your back-home mindset
  12. Spark wanderlust: travel vicariously
  13. Getting there and back: consider the possibilities
  14. Bring a journey home: the tangible and intangible
  15. What to share with others: what to cherish for yourself

Trusting Your Senses: **Page 61**

16. Magic: just outside the kitchen window
17. Frame your experience: see through the camera's lens
18. Capture the moment: your eyes or others' eyes
19. Smell: re-awakening a most primitive sense
20. The sound of silence: deliberate disengagement
21. Body language skills: fine-tune the unspoken dialogue

Shifting Perspectives: mindfulness in action   **Page 83**

22. How travel augments therapy: leave the couch behind
23. Travel as therapy: shift your mindset wherever you go
24. Quiet yourself: downshift the gears
25. Positive psychology: enjoying yourself is a state of mind
26. Be here now: manage your attention
27. Increase life's intensity: compress time
28. Follow your curiosity: novelty and creativity
29. Empathy: a walk in others' shoes

Managing Risk and Change: spin a positive scenario   **Page 113**

30. Adventure or risk? Ocean kayaking
31. Escape the beaten path: wilderness travel
32. Start over: try on a new you
33. Social stretching: travel to meet people
34. The threat of danger: successful coping
35. When the unanticipated happens: choose how to respond
36. Return to health: how travel planning gets you there
37. Find the good: manage disappointment and unrealistic expectations

Making Choices   **Page 143**

38. Choose between competing goals
39. Set aside cravings: alternative scenarios to make travel work
40. Fine-tune your needs: quicken or slow the pace?
41. Feed your passion or curiosity: travel with a specific theme
42. Solo travel: new behavior or preferred approach
43. Shared travel: deepen good relationships or renew stale ones
44. Travel following loss: find wellsprings of comfort and peace

Mind and Emotions at Work   **Page 169**

45. Introvert or extravert: navigate the journey your own way
46. Overcome self-perceived limitations
47. Expand your tastes and preferences
48. How time perspective affects travel: do you live in the past, present or future?
49. Travel impacts the brain and psyche: modify your brain's structure and function
50. The benefits of a distracted mind: when focus gets in the way
51. Success increases confidence: an adventure in baby steps

Some Final Thoughts   **Page 197**

Quiz: Find Your Travel Style   **Page 201**

Acknowledgements   **Page 205**

Appendix: Places Mentioned   **Page 207**

Introduction

Humans are an inquisitive species and we yearn to know about the only planet we can personally explore—whether it's near to home or around the globe. Much more than physical movement, taking in the local sights, or even acknowledging the awesomeness of nature, we travel to experience newness, to satisfy our curiosity about the world, and to understand its people and cultures.

The *Inward Traveler* offers a series of adventures big and small, near and far, but always designed to make every moment richer and more mindfully experienced. From the smells wafting toward you from the Istanbul spice market, to the stark and wind swept tip of southern Chile, and to the dead-silent mountain tops on the island of Kauai, each stand-alone mini-chapter takes you on a journey to explore your inner thoughts, feelings and sensations while investigating the world that surrounds you.

Whether your travels take you across an ocean or just across a street, the *Inward Traveler* provides ways to sense the world deeply and in the present moment—which may require a slight shift from the busy and somewhat distracted daily patterns that characterize the 21st century lifestyle. But you'll find prompts in each of the following chapters to guide you.

Not a traditional travel book recommending places and providing logistics about packing or where to eat, the *Inward Traveler* provides cues to enrich any experience through the process of heightened attention and immersion in experiences. Through travel stories, anecdotes and metaphors, we'll explore the process of living fully—

and in the moment, through journeys of any size. An aging psychologist and seasoned traveler guides your experiences as well as *your inner reactions to your outward travels*.

Making the most of travel is what this book is all about. It's a tech manual that teaches you how to bathe in positive experiences encountered as well as ways to deal with the trials and tribulations encountered along the way. By conscious reframing you'll also learn how to alleviate some of the problems or stresses in life, while substituting positive feelings.

Journeys need not be limited to the long weekend, two-week summer vacation, or once in a lifetime journey. In the following pages you'll learn to extend your wanderer mindset to capture any moment and see how such shifts can lead to novel getaways. In the chapters that follow, you'll find a template for capturing life more fully as you live it.

Being present, in the exact instant when you notice your heart beating and the sensation of inhaling fresh air, requires conscious intent or training for most of us. Staying fully present is challenging. In-the-moment experiences easily get derailed by what's happening next as well as nostalgia about the day before.

Living life in the future and the past is generally so comfortable for us that the present can become a mere conduit from past to future. We make elaborate plans, spend loads of money and anticipate all sorts of scenarios about the places we hope to visit. But planning for what comes next, distracts from the only moment that truly exists. Now!

The *Inward Traveler* guides the reader's exploration of the world mindfully, meaningfully and fully, through examples, metaphors, and easy to follow exercises.

How this book came about:

You'd think that being a psychologist for more than half a century might have provided me with all the answers to life's questions, or at least a lot of them. And yet, in spite of the passage of so many years, something still seemed missing. So my journey as an *inward traveler* continued and led to the writing of this book which helped me further unravel the complex and enormous puzzle we call life.

Fortunately, two different but compatible philosophies surfaced during the past couple of decades that impacted my thinking about life and the writing of this book. The first influence, called *applied Buddhism*, is a translation of ancient eastern philosophy into practices that are designed to calm and center our restless souls. It includes a powerful strategy called *mindfulness*.

The second influence, *positive psychology*, emerged from the field of behavioral psychology to embrace what is *good* and *right* in our life just the way it is. Psychologists, as you probably know, have traditionally attended mostly to what's wrong, missing, painful and pathological, relying on the medical model for curing disease and returning people to a neutral baseline that remediates pain and suffering. But the upside, the place of optimal/ideal functioning (beyond a neutral baseline) is finally getting some attention. Seeing what's right, beautiful, pleasurable and awe inspiring in the world can elude us in our contemporary, chaotic and increasingly dangerous surroundings. Both Buddhism and Positive Psychology helped refine my ideas about experiencing a life well lived.

Positive psychology, was first introduced by Martin Seligman, Ph.D., professor of psychology at the University of Pennsylvania, in a special issue of the *American Psychologist* journal (January, 2000) dedicated to "Happiness, Excellence and Optimal Human Functioning."

That particular journal issue was an extraordinary way to usher in the new millennium because of its departure from the negative territory that psychology had dwelled in since the days of Sigmund Freud. In an introductory statement, Seligman wrote, "The exclusive focus on pathology that has dominated so much of our discipline results in a model of the human being lacking the positive features that make life worth living. Hope, wisdom, creativity, … are ignored or explained as transformations of more authentic negative impulses."

The *Inward Traveler* focuses on the "upside" of psychological functioning ushered in by the positive psychology movement, which has been thoroughly researched and popularized in the past two decades.

In that same journal article, psychologist, Mihaly Csikszentmihalyi, then a professor at the University of Chicago, presented the concept known as *flow*, based on his book of the same name, *Flow* (1990). In it he says, "Happiness is not something that happens. It is not the result of good fortune or random chance. It is not something that money can buy or power command. It does not depend on outside events, but, rather, on how we interpret them.… People who learn to control inner experience will be able to determine the quality of their lives, which is as close as any of us can come to being happy." So, focus on our inner experience to enhance the quality of life, will be the backbone of the *Inward Traveler*. You will see elements of both positive psychology and flow woven into the chapters that follow.

It's been years since I closed my psychotherapy practice and no longer have responsibility for helping others travel the rocky road of life from suffering to increased emotional and psychological health. But having my own unfinished business propelled me forward through mindfulness and positive approaches as I applied them to my own life.

With more travel time, fewer external obligations, and the luxury that comes with aging and relatively good health—I wondered, "what's next." I'm in good company here. Herman Wouck, the Pulitzer prize winning author of more than ten books, most notably *The Winds of War* and *The Caine Mutiny*, just turned 100 years old and recently completed a memoir about his more than 75 years as a writer living in the most dynamic time in the world's history. Even he wonders about what comes next. With his jobs all done, he wonders what now? He remains curious and open to new experience, an excellent elder role model—which is comforting.

Similarly, the British psychiatrist, Oliver Sacks, author of more than 15 books, wrote about the wisdom that comes with aging in his memoir composed at the end of his 86th year. Just when we think we've been there, done that, a new chapter opens.

I got the idea for the *Inward Traveler* years ago while vacationing in an often visited spot—northern Kauai, Hawaii. While the sights were familiar enough to picture with closed eyes, I realized there was more—not places, but ways to see, feel, and think about them. And I began to blog about these ideas which also satisfied my writer's urge. The passage of time with wider travels further expanded my ideas and blossomed into this book. Have a wonderful journey.

Photo 1: Far north coastline, Kauai, Hawaii

Traditions and viewpoints

Introduction

How we experience a journey depends on *how* we approach it, including the many ways we infuse it with personal meaning. This section of The *Inward Traveler* explores some underpinnings derived from Eastern philosophy and a framework of **positivity** and **flow** to further enhance any journey. It highlights the *how* rather than the *where* of travel. It offers a variety of viewpoints that have enriched world travelers throughout history.

Travel satisfies our wanderlust. Like a kaleidoscopic view, all places are dynamic, ever changing shapes altered by the passage of time, mother nature, cultures, and the people who call the location home. These factors may sum up the usual elements guiding our choice of a destination. But, what most affects our take-away is the lens through which we view, and the framework that binds, our experiences together.

Illustration 1: Kaleidoscope and meditative mandala

Buddhist and Tao principles: novel ways to meditate

"No matter where you go, there you are." This timeless and much quoted saying attributed to Confucius, an ancient Chinese philosopher and teacher, suggests that you can't escape from your mindset and emotions. Eastern philosophies infuse and guide the *Inward Traveler's* explorations near and far.

Whether Buddhist, Tao or Zen, these ways of seeing the world focus on the interplay among physical body, thoughts/feelings and the environment. You can adapt and apply the philosophy as-is or tailor its teachings to suit your life. In whatever ways you choose to use these Eastern ideas, your journeys will surely be enhanced. This chapter is all about the *how* of travel rather than the *where*.

The word *Buddha* literally translates as "awaken," which suggests that staying aware in the moment is to be like the Buddha—awake and acutely sensing each moment. This is why all of the Eastern traditions focus on your breath and ways to anchor you to the present. Breathing works like background music—surfacing when you pay attention to it. And at that instant everything else fades as it does when an entrancing piece of music captures your attention. Even if only for a few seconds, a time-out from all but breathing lets you center and soothe your body and psyche.

You don't have to sit and meditate or take a yoga class to make this happen, but it can help because with few distractions other than the movement of your body, it's easier to notice your breathing. Controlled by your autonomic nervous system, beyond your conscious control, inhaling and exhaling maintain life and give it rhythm whether you're paying attention or not. For example, altering the length of your exhalation helps bring your focus to the here and now, and away from an endless to-do list and other concerns. That's called *conscious breathing*.

But staying still and noticing your breathing isn't for everyone. For those of us who have trouble with this idea, there is always moving meditation. Any movement can be performed as a meditation with mindfulness and a slow pace. Focus centers on the motions themselves rather than any practical goal such as walking to a specific destination. In some Eastern traditions the walk is guided by a mandala on the ground which is like a never ending circle designed to be visually appealing.

Not keen on walking in circles? Consider the numerous coloring books made up of page-sized, intricately designed mandalas waiting for your crayons. You can think of the mandala as a dynamic, energy packed symbol, a pathway to creative expression through filling the spaces on a sheet of paper with color. You personally choose the hues which makes it a perfect starting point for someone who feels challenged by the visual arts.

Or you might find a labyrinth. Known as walking mandalas, labyrinths blend their visual symbolism with the process of walking. The most famous of these is in Chartres Cathedral in northern France, which was constructed during the second decade of the 13th century. It makes a great destination or side trip to balance a hectic travel itinerary. But you needn't go this far to find one. Many religious traditions have adopted the idea of tranquility and inner peace associated with labyrinth walking. There might even be a labyrinth-like site in your own neighborhood. Some parks, libraries and churches have incorporated these in their landscaping.

The Taoist tradition, still another Eastern philosophy, has a slightly different emphasis than Buddhism. It provides a *spiritual* path that goes beyond having a calm, peaceful mind. Taoist meditation makes you aware of the permanent, unchanging center of your being. So while time passes, and the environment changes, and the human body itself mirrors the seasons from Spring to Winter—your core (body, spirit) remains steady, like an anchor in a rough sea according to Tao.

If you follow the Tao, you can maintain equilibrium even when the metaphorical seas are rough. You may even find internal quiet to better manage the push and pull of daily life. You might even free your creative process from internal clutter.

Because life itself is a journey, the *Inward Traveler* can focus mindfully on any moment and find meaning and peace there. Let your mindful journey begin with your breath, a walk, or a coloring book.

Yoga and Tai Chi: take meditation on the road

The old saying, "You can't take it with you" doesn't apply here and these travel friendly practices won't add any weight to your baggage. Traveling can strain even the most seasoned wanderer. But the following time-tested remedies can help without any side effects.

Yoga and tai chi provide comfort as well as exercise while on the road. Aside from the physical benefits, there's the sense of peacefulness and deepened awareness of time and place to enhance what you see, hear and feel along the way. That's perfect for the *Inward Traveler* who chooses to be fully present.

Experiencing moment-to-moment awareness of your thoughts and feelings without judgment is the common goal of yoga—a form of *moving* meditation. Learn to heighten your senses and enhance whatever you experience—wherever it is. Combine this with rhythmic breathing and you've created a dynamic and enlivening process that's been around for eons. Incidentally, this is a skill cultivated by athletes to enhance their performance. It incorporates the notions of *mindfulness* and *flow*.

In the mid-twentieth century, meditation, yoga, and tai chi came out of the temples of Asia and the churches and cloistered monasteries of Europe infusing American culture and lifestyle with a new way to center the body and quiet the mind. But what does this have to do with travel?

Wherever you go you'll likely find a yoga class or a group of intensely focused adults practicing martial-arts-based and dance-like tai chi moves in a public place like a grassy municipal park. A series of graceful movements, once learned, can help you fit into a tai chi group anywhere.

Language is not a barrier for yoga or tai chi since both depend on the natural movements of the human body and neither requires speaking. Whether around the corner where you live or half-way around the world, take your practice with you and join a group if it meets your need for contact with others.

But my own introverted nature prefers a solo yoga practice and when I arrive at a new destination and feel sleepy it works better than a cup of coffee. Yoga postures, like the familiar *downward facing dog*, (see Illustration 2) reduce tension when practiced slowly. Intentionally accentuate your out-breath and practice sighing out loud as you do. Having a ridiculously audible groan actually helps to further counter weariness.

Alternatively, when I'm sleep deprived and jet lagged, moving *quickly* and doing several repetitions of a sequence like *salutation to the sun* (see Illustration 2) wake me up and keep me alert for hours until I can take advantage of the next local sleep cycle. Try some yoga postures. Let Illustration 2 guide you to try *downward facing dog* and the *salutation to the sun* sequence. All you really need is a carpeted floor and a dose of curiosity.

Unless you are a yogi or meditation master, your thoughts are bound to wander during your practice. Expect that to happen and then simply remind yourself to breathe. Try not to critically judge the content of your thoughts, or yourself for thinking them. Even positive judgments—liking or enjoying something, can alter your actual experience. Judging actually diminishes the experience—because it distracts from the peace of *now*. So catch yourself and let any such thoughts float away.

Illustration 2: Yoga sequence called "salutation to the sun." Pose #5 is called "downward facing dog"

Associated with such varied traditions as Tibetan, Chinese, Indian, Christian, Jewish or Moslem, meditative practices begin by simply following the breath. Most religions see the value of deepening spirituality by using exaggerated breathing, chanting or a mantra to keep you centered.

A mantra can be a sound or a word that keeps you focused by wrapping your attention around it to help block other thoughts. You're probably already familiar with the sound of "Om." Find your own sound—or make one up that's pleasing to your ears, and doesn't get you thinking about other things. But most important, remember to take your practice on your journeys. Find space and privacy.

Photo 2: Tai Chi practice in a park setting

Awe: Seeing life with a beginner's mind

The *beginner's mind* is a state of wonder and curiosity lost to many of us when we emerge from childhood. This ancient Buddhist premise relies on openness to experience not colored by our own expectations, preconceived notions, or stereotypic ideas. Think about how a young child approaches a new experience. It's with an open and inquisitive mind without biases or goals.

As an *Inward Traveler* I know the importance of taking a fresh approach to seeing something new and unfamiliar, without putting it into a container filled with personal history and baggage. I wish I could do that more often. I'd like to simply roam and encounter whatever I encounter along the way, as opposed to seeing places in a tightly bound package of routine or habitual stuff. I decided to give myself this opportunity on an extended trip to South America, and here's what happened.

One sun drenched Sunday I wandered through a typical Ecuadorian marketplace in a small coastal city called Manta—mostly known for its tuna packing plant. Some mesmerizing music drew me toward it as if I were in a trance. The haunting sound of the Andes Mountains found expression through some traditional pan-pipe melodies. The musician was a young man with a selection of flutes and pipes in different sizes adorning a red and orange woven cloth atop the table that separated us.[1]

The flutist, dark skinned and petite, resembled the indigenous population of South American Indios in his appearance: a colorfully

---

[1] See photo on page 198.

woven shirt, and a feathered hat typical of the Andes Mountains. He tracked my eyes and picked up an instrument that held my gaze and began to play, almost in response to the question in my mind, as yet un-verbalized.

We connected without language, and I watched how he played this new-to-me instrument so that I could try to do the same. He spoke no English, but saw the fascination in my intense stare and gently swaying body. The marketplace attracts many locals and tourists focused on buying souvenirs or household necessaries but most seemed indifferent to the music as a focus—more like background or white noise perhaps. Not so for me!

I indicated that I wanted to buy one, and pointed to a small wooden pipe, without speaking a word and he understood. We even agreed on a price—all this without shared language. I tried some Spanish and English. He responded in an unfamiliar dialect. Neither of us had any ideas what the other was saying. We both seemed to thoroughly enjoy the transaction and the social exchange that depended exclusively on non-verbal cues.

Our interaction was playful, unanticipated, unstructured and well outside of the box I usually create for new experiences. Play, unlike work, has no goal outside of itself. Play is childlike, open, and curious with no fixed rules. Entering into this new situation with a "beginner's mind" led to the unexpected: seeing, feeling, hearing, and sensing whatever was available at the moment. It was full of wonder but a bit uncomfortable because of its unfamiliarity to my grown-up nature.

When I realized that I wandered away from my group and was lost in music, a bit of embarrassment crept in which I caught in time to stifle. I did my best to let the disquiet go and get back to playing. But being an overly-socialized adult my internal dialogue did include bits of evaluation, judgment and criticism. Oh, well, I'm still a work in progress!

Can you push the boundaries of your own experience by adopting a *beginner's mind*? Can you stay aware of any judgments, limiting thoughts or uncomfortable feelings that get in the way of trying new experiences? What will you need to change in yourself to make this possible? Will the grown-up tendency to compare (better than, worse than) or perform (success or failure) pop up? Remember, whether traveling near or far, a central goal of the *Inward Traveler* is mindfulness about one's own internal process.

At the local level, pick a place within ten miles of your home to try this experiment. Look at a regional map and find a spot unfamiliar to you: a small town, nature spot, landmark or anything else that captures your attention. Plan a "trip" there for a few hours or a half-day. With an *Inward Traveler's* mindset this experience will be as much about a change from one state of mind to another as it is about going someplace new. Remember, no rules—just play and, of course, suspend judgment.

Wonder: where the oceans meet

There's only one place in the world where the Atlantic and Pacific Oceans converge. It's at Cape Horn, Chile—the most southern point of land on the planet that is not Antarctica. On my voyage around South America I couldn't wait to see the exact point where the two oceans met. What did I expect? I genuinely anticipated some kind of fanfare like different currents, a shift in the hue of blue water, or maybe the size of waves. I somehow needed to understand or explain to myself how the physical world works and why two oceans would actually touch, and yet be different and have separate names. These kinds of things matter to me, and maybe to you as well.

It turns out that the line between the two oceans is arbitrary and specified mostly for the benefit of oceanographers, adventurers, or passing ocean vessels filled with gawking tourists like myself— though there really are temperature differences between the two water masses, which clearly weren't visible.

I like the notion that the oceans belong to all of us, not as they are carved up by nations or people anxious to possess chunks of the earth. The earliest people appreciated the splendor of their physical environment, even attributing spiritual significance to the earth's bounty. These days, humans may be far removed from even noticing the extraordinary supply chain that begins with the features of the land itself. But reconnecting might be just a trip away. This is why travel to Cape Horn seemed to hold intrigue for me.

Cape Horn is undoubtedly the most sparsely populated tourist destination in the world Four residents, to be exact, live there temporarily. The site has one building—a lighthouse. It's inhabited by a Chilean naval officer, along with his wife and two children. Their four-month commitment to a bare rock, too inhospitable for trees or animals of any size, seems daunting. Once a week provisions arrive by supply ship from the mainland and they're hoisted by hand pulley to the top of the mountain outcropping called home. The wind blows at 50 mph. But the pay is good. When their term is over another individual or family curious about extreme living will arrive. Would you do it?

What is it about the land itself that beckons some of us to search for experience in even the most severe settings? Most of us won't climb Mt. Everest, but human curiosity, and the quest for adventure outside of the routine, seems universal. Is it our desire to make some kind of sense out of our connection to the universe? Is it the restoration we feel when we take the time to notice and plunge deep within the grandeur of the one planet we can call home? This is the integration of inner and global travel.

Seeing Cape Horn's extraordinary but forbidding setting and its stark life-style reminds me that we humans have different tolerances and varying degrees of comfort in unusual situations. Being in an extreme setting like this gave me a chance to rule in and rule out what's necessary for a satisfying life and what gives me pleasure. How would you assess your own tolerance for this kind of situation?

Photo 3: Ushuaia, Argentina is the southernmost city in the world and gateway to Antarctica for icebreaker ships.

If extreme nature has no appeal for you, consider the majesty in the grand design of a sprawling meadow—a beauty with tall golden grasses that sway gently in the early autumn breeze. Such a place provides for the necessities of life in the form of grain that's harvested for food. An ice capped mountain has its own splendor, like a jewel in the sky, but it also provides clean water for survival in the valley below. Take the time to appreciate these natural and timeless wonders that feed our soul and sustain our bodies.

Contemplative Journeys: walking meditation—virtual and real

What is the advantage of walking meditation as opposed to simply taking a walk alone with one's thoughts? The value is in its very repetitive movement, one foot meditatively placed in front of the other, but without any end goal or place to go. The repetitive process can be soothing, centering, quieting. It's ideal for fidgety folks who can't sit still—like me!

Walking meditation is travel without a particular destination but with a focus and concentration on simply being—not the distractions and reactions of life. You can incorporate this practice in your garden, the city streets you walk on a daily basis, or by hiking anywhere in the world.

Virtual experience: Take a virtual walk with me—using only your imagination: Create a paved path in your mind. This makes it easier to move without much conscious thought about where you're headed or whether there will be obstacles underfoot that threaten your safety. The hike is a loop making it difficult to get lost. That's what you're looking for in an ideal route.

Now we're on the virtual path which doesn't need to be remote and may have other walkers including humans and animals, flyers including birds and planes, diggers including squirrels and moles and the occasional grazing deer. Sounds abound and fill the ears. Delightful foliage or awful blight may be part of the scene. All of these become powerful distractors if you choose to notice and then get caught up in thinking about them.

Take a moment to acknowledge your virtual observations. If, in fact, you do notice sounds, sensations, and sights, quickly let them go and return to focus on your breathing—otherwise you risk sidetracking your walking meditation. There's great temptation in taking in what we notice and going on tangents by telling ourselves stories that take us away for the moment.

Notice only what's essential to this time and place: your breath and your foot steps, both forming patterns. Feel and listen to your continuous in and out breaths, feel them in your upper body, experience the movement of your legs and the sound of your feet or shoes making contact with the path. Come back to these sensations when your busy mind takes your away.

Over and over, for as long as the walk takes, your conscious mind returns to your bodily experiences as they propel your inner journey toward your outward experience. Now you are back where you started and while you've gone nowhere, you may feel different—lighter, more energized or more peaceful.

For thousands of years, contemplative journeys by foot have offered calming and therapeutic outcomes. Meditation is a tradition that usually depends on stillness of the mind and body, which most Westerners find difficult to imagine, no less execute. Walking meditation is a compromise, surprisingly easy to learn. Patience is the key to its success.

Hatha yoga is an ancient tradition, involving body movement but a quiet mind, dating back to sometime between the 5th and 11th century C.E. It includes the practice of *asanas* (postures), coordinated with *pranayama* (breathing practices). Coordinating body movement with a focus on our inner state of being provides a new quality of experience to enrich each moment.

One familiar example of how this works is "downward facing dog," mentioned in an earlier chapter. It's a posture that requires the body to remain still in a particular pattern resembling a down stretched dog, while at the same time paying attention to breathing in and out.

The ultimate goal of yoga practice is to bring peace to the body and mind, while preparing the body for deeper spiritual practices such as meditation. Put the two practices together and you get walking meditation: movement combined with a focus on breathing, or at least being mindful of what you *are* thinking and feeling, so that you can return to your breathing each time your attention wavers.

The virtual journey is over. Time to practice with the real thing. It's your turn!

Photo 4: Yoga posture: tree pose

Heighten personal meaning through travel

Seeking to enhance meaning in life is part of the human experience—especially as evoked around 1) life transitions like graduation, marriage, divorce, or retirement; 2) the aging process and the questions it raises about mortality; 3) grieving and recovering from a loss.

Meaning is a highly individualized process that evokes different thoughts and emotions in each of us. Meaning might feel inseparable from religion—for some of us. If that is true for you, the natural segue might be a journey to a monastery, temple or mosque. It's easy to identify tours that specialize in this kind of travel, sometimes known as pilgrimages. If that's the type of meaning you crave, the options are explicit and well defined, and easy to identify. See "Making Choices" for examples.

But meaning might be more broadly defined and nebulous for you, not necessarily tied to religious quests or beliefs. Enhanced meaning might even be a byproduct of more fully understanding how the world or universe works. Here's an example from my own travels.

While on a cruise from Lisbon, Portugal to Barcelona, Spain via the straits of Gibraltar, I knew that the ship would be passing from the Atlantic Ocean into the Mediterranean Sea. Yes, I am obsessively curious about oceans! I didn't know exactly where or when the precise point would be. I wondered if there would be a difference in the presence or absence of sea life. I looked out for any phenomenon that would serve as a cue—like giant sea turtles.

While I waited for information that might confirm the line of demarcation between the two bodies of water, I thought about how the seas are interconnected and how life itself emerged from the sea. I thought about other imprecise ways of knowing when something changes into something else—day into dusk and then darkness, summer into fall, an interest into an obsession, adolescence into adulthood.

In this journey called life, finding the meaning in things can happen as casually as my search for a marker in the sea! Incidentally, I never did see a shift from one body of water to the next. But I did have fun while I imagined it. It got me thinking about how change can be so gradual that it happens seamlessly or barely visibly.

How might your search for meaning lead to travel, or your travel spark a search for meaning? For starters, meaning can be derived from any observation or situation, but the key is to take the time to reflect, to pause and ask questions and have the time and patience to fully absorb the hints and answers.

Going to your ancestral home to learn about your family's culture in the old country certainly can infuse your trip with meaning—getting a picture of where you belong in the long line that shares your DNA. But a nearby experience might include trekking to a local old cemetery and reading the gravestone inscriptions. While less personally relevant, this experience can be equally meaningful as it evokes awareness of markers in the life cycle, and your own perceptions of life and death. Whichever you choose, it gives you a context for exploring a life-line.

There's no shortage of outings to whet your appetite for meaning. Other ideas might include viewing the night sky via a telescope or a trip to a nearby planetarium. Both of these excursions can create wonder about the vastness or the universe and your place in it. Visiting an aquarium might spark your curiosity about how life itself evolved from the sea.

Travel, whether just around the block or to distant places, gives an opportunity to consciously choose to notice—not just see, but fully immerse all the senses in what is happening. Once again, we are talking about *mindfulness* and *flow*.

According to, Professor Mihaly Csikszentmihalyi, author of *Flow*, "subjective experience is not just one of the dimensions of life, it *is* life itself." And "the process of total involvement with life I call *flow*.... Concentration is so intense that there is no attention left over to think about anything irrelevant, or to worry about problems....and the sense of time becomes distorted. An activity that produces such experiences is so gratifying that people are willing to do it for its own sake, with little concern for what they will get out of it, even when it is difficult or dangerous."

Travel by definition is planned, not accidental, so it takes you out of the ordinary day to day mindset and, all too often, repetitive activities. It can be challenging or comfortable. Meaning can be sought or discovered anywhere and quite by accident. You may find it where you least expect it—the trick is to immerse yourself in your senses and notice.

This section of the book introduced you to traditions and viewpoints to help you achieve mindfulness and flow as you travel through your life with the greatest satisfaction.

Maximizing Travel: before, during, and afterwards

Introduction

Make more of any and all journeys. Enrich your life and brighten your observations of the past, present and future. Expand your adventure as far as your imagination and attention can take it. This section of the book points to the experiences that precede and follow travel in addition to real-time moments. A trip is time limited but a journey can extend well beyond a fixed point in time. Learn how to optimize any voyage in the following nine mini-chapters.

Photo 5: A cruise ship arrives at the harbor in Santorini, Greece

Enhance your experience *beforehand*: positive anticipation

Savoring a trip in advance is a bonus that intensifies pleasant emotion. From the moment you begin to imagine the trip until you begin your journey, whether days, weeks, months or years away, you can psychologically benefit from tasting what you anticipate in advance. Let thoughts about your trip float into consciousness when your mind wanders. Welcome and nurture what comes as long as it doesn't habitually distract from your task at hand.

As I'm attempting to write about something else, an upcoming visit to the coast comes to mind. I imagine the waves breaking on large outcroppings in the wild waters of northern California. I can even taste the salt water mist while walking along the cliffs. It's a foggy early morning with a chill in the air. In my imagination I brace against headwinds by folding my arms across my body and tightly wrapping my wind breaker. As I walk back to my rustic but cozy lodging, cold but invigorated, I look forward to a steaming hot mug of coffee that I can wrap both hands around.

Then I catch myself in this delightful diversion. I know that it meets my emotional needs but not my writing goals. I allowed the thought to wash over me even when I became aware of what I was doing. It helped momentarily to distract from the task at hand—writing. But as we shall learn in a later section (The Mind and Emotions at Work), distraction can actually serve as an incubator and aid the creative process.

We usually associate a trip's pleasure and meaning with the actual experience, replaying it in our mind afterwards, recalling it via pictures and conversations. Yet, an old friend once said that the pleasure of travel begins with planning, and that takes place way ahead of of the journey. I believe it's true!

Learn how to use positive anticipation as a stimulus for creative thinking. Begin to identify which anticipatory thoughts and feelings enhance your goals and which serve simply to divert you when the going gets tough. Recognize your motivation and decide whether to indulge in the daydream because it's good for you at this moment or set it aside for a designated time slot when you can fully enjoy the virtual experience, without feeling guilty. But do make the time! Why leave that process to chance?

Be proactive in your approach. Daydreaming about a future journey, extended or brief, may not simply happen by itself. Consider planting reminders in your environment to cue your trip. Focus on the features that seem most rewarding. Hang a travel brochure on your bulletin board, for example, or place a link in your electronic device's "favorites." Both cues are good first steps. You might spend some time with early planning, making a list of the things you'd like to bring and add to it when your mind wanders to your upcoming travel. The more reminders you place around you, and the more often you access these clues, the more pleasure you'll feel.

Why is this important? Just as you anticipate the taste of a good piece of chocolate, or any other food of your choice, the process of positively anticipating a trip also begins with a thought. You won't begin to salivate, the way you might before a special desert, but if you've ever enjoyed an actual trip then contemplating an upcoming trip will evoke similarly positive sensations.

Let's say you have a trip planned. What can you do to increase your good feelings in the moment about an event that may still be quite far away in time? Can you make the lead-up an integral part of the trip experience?

- The planning and preparation serves to prolong the positive effects and enhances the actual outcome.
- Take the time to daydream about the specifics.
- Read a novel set in the place you'll visit.
- Find a movie or travelogue to watch about your destination.

Put yourself in the mind-frame virtually and then trust your creation.

You can have a short vacation without short-changing yourself

The United States has a notorious reputation for offering its workforce some of the shortest number of vacation days per year. Compared to Western Europe our cultural work ethic is bit extreme. But even more striking is the statistic that each year thousands of hours of vacation time get shelved, unspent.

Almost like a badge of honor, Americans take less time than they are entitled to. Proving what? That we are serious workers in our own minds, or invaluable to our organization? Maybe it's a competitive thing or based on fear of seeming like a slacker. Or worse, worries about being replaced. Whatever the cause, the effect limits our pleasure and ultimately reduces workplace effectiveness.

R & R is a necessity, not a guilty indulgence but you'd never know that from watching how most of us live. This book won't change employers' time-off policies but the quality of the time you do take is not dependent on that. Even a brief getaway can be savored. Here's an example.

Having just returned from an overnight trip up the Pacific coast about 100 miles, I'm baffled that I didn't make this happen sooner. Inflexible thinking about what is possible can become a limiting factor. We can get boxed in by stilted logic and myopic planning. That's exactly what happened to me.

Nearly a year ago I received a gift certificate for a particular lodge in Bodega Bay, California that sits at the edge of land hugging the wild Pacific coast. The certificate sat in a kitchen drawer waiting for the ideal time—which of course never came. While I searched for two consecutive nights that worked in my current schedule, and would be covered by the gift certificate, I remained at a loss.

As long as I clung to my belief that a minimum of two nights somehow defined a trip, it just couldn't happen—that is, with other time commitments. If desperation is truly the mother of invention, then it worked to free me to consider an alternative. It occurred to me that just one night away might be a solution. Why not spend the money that remained on the gift card on something other than lodging, like an upscale dinner? That's just what I did and it turned out wonderfully.

Making the most of the newly found opportunity, I greedily devoured colorful, glossy brochures. I imagined more pleasant scenarios than I could ever cram into two days, but it sure satisfied my appetite for wanderlust.

Hiking the cliffs that bracket Bodega Bay offered tactile rewards like salt spray carried by the wind from the crashing waves below and some visual pleasures like seeing vigilant pelicans focus and then dive for fish with bullet speed.

The craggy rock outcroppings in shades of red and brown arranged in horizontal stripes revealed its age in geological years. The sounds of sea lions barking in the waters below added an aural dimension to this dynamic and mesmerizing scene.

Accepting the idea that a one-night hotel stay sandwiched between two days of exploring was perfectly reasonable, led to some delicious, positive anticipation. In retrospect, I remember this overnighter as one of my favorite getaways.

Photo 6: The cliffs at Bodega Head, Bodega Bay, California

Wherever you live, it's likely that there's natural beauty nearby; architecture that sparks curiosity or admiration and interesting day trips. Brief trips are within your grasp when you take the time to look at your extended community, or neighboring places. Think about your own personal orientation to the world, starting with your current interests. History buff? Art enthusiast? Water lover? Hiker? There's something for everyone.

Approach the process as you would any trip. Start with a tourist map highlighting features that make your place special. Using the internet, research what the local chamber of commerce highlights as charming and significant.

But here's the disclaimer. Occasionally taking time off makes returning to work an unpleasant catch-up ordeal. Or there might be other anticipated hassles like finding a baby or dog sitter, which are certainly valid reasons to table a vacation that feels costly, financially or otherwise. Don't rule out an overnighter or "staycation." This is a handy concept that helps to reduce the cost and annoyance factor. Whether taking a week or long weekend off, keep in mind that merely staying home and maintaining the same daily patterns won't satisfy your needs.

To have a restful, relaxing or meaningful experience requires a vacation mindset, even in your own home. It also requires some planning. Don't forget to shake up the routine.

Reframe the question: "Can I afford to take time off?" Wonder instead:

- How can I make it happen?
- Find ways to implement a plan without limiting your creativity.
- Suspend the rules and notice your judgments about what is possible or not.

You might just surprise and delight yourself.

Transportation hassles: reframe your experience

There was a time when getting to a destination seemed glamorous or even romantic. Airline travel was elegant in the days when stewardesses wore white gloves, high heels and hats while they served free cocktails. Train travel once evoked images of the Orient Express from Constantinople to Paris, replete with intrigue, mystery and charm. Ship travel a half-century ago had the glitz and pageantry of royal coronations.

Today, thanks partially to various dangers around the globe, getting anywhere and back is aggravating at best. Long lines, security, searches and limits on what or how much you can transport make coming and going a pain. Since your travel is book-marked by getting there and returning home, finding ways to maintain your sanity, sense of humor, and a positive mood takes some doing. While you hopefully have time to undo the negativity associated with the outbound experience, the final trek home has the power to spoil almost an entire journey.

Psychological research supports the idea that memories depend heavily on what's last experienced in a series of events. What that means is that the last event in a vacation can color the entire experience. If that is so, frustrating airport encounters have the potential to degrade, or at least tarnish, memories of a lovely vacation.

I recall leaving Kauai, Hawaii, one late night for a red eye flight to California. Still infused with the magical island glow, I arrived with a crowd of others at a small airport, jostled along into the agricultural inspection line where my banana was confiscated, followed by full-metal security check. After two weeks of paradise, I was thrust back into my tense pre-trip state of mind.

I felt irritable, tense, and felt my pulse rate quicken. I was herded, pushed and shoved by other passengers guarding their bodies, personal space and possessions as they carved out meager space for themselves in a crowded queue.

Desperate for help with ways to maintain the inner glow, in spite of transportation annoyances, I tried to remember what I'd learned from psychological research about ways to salvage *positivity*. It's not easy to do, but we have more control over our thoughts and how we see things than we imagine. While the last encounter does have strong potential to influence memories, it's not the only factor. Your job is to retrieve other memories, just as powerful but much more pleasant, and focus your attention on these. Try to remember what was good. It's tough when you're annoyed but worth the effort.

You can also alter your unpleasant feelings by altering your physiology. When your body tenses, your brain gets a message that there is some kind of danger present—though it's not like a face-to-face encounter with a hungry beast that your distant ancestors might have confronted as they left their cave.

When your breathing is shallow your brain assumes that you're not feeling safe. Your brain is pre-programmed to take what is known as a *flight or fight* posture which in turn further tightens your muscles, increases your heart rate, and braces you for some fearful encounter. Of course, there is no *real* danger—no monster at the cave entrance.

But what you want is a reversal of this process so that your brain senses peacefulness and begins to release tension in your body. You can make this happen by slowing your breathing and focusing on the flow of air as you inhale through your nostrils and as it flows to various parts of your body. Continue to imagine tension flowing out of your body with each exhalation. Think back to the Eastern philosophies in the first section of this book: breathe.

That's exactly what I did when the airline check-in situation threatened to upset my good time; and while it wasn't like floating down a river in an inner tube, it did help. Focusing on the previous pleasant days, and on the fact that I could influence my own reaction to the unpleasantness at the airport, did make a difference. It's your turn to practice this restorative breathing—best done before you actually need to use it.

Trust your instinct, judgment, and experience

Exploring new places takes us out of our comfort zone which can feel disorienting. When we're away from what we know and take for granted that can feel like being in a rowboat without oars. But a new encounter doesn't have to be a stressful or negative experience. Quite the contrary. You might just learn about strengths and skills you didn't know you had. Here's an example.

Imagine driving one evening, from your hotel to a new adventure. You have the address for an unfamiliar destination and the drive is pleasant and uneventful, that is, until you pass into an area that gradually becomes foggy. You hope that it will clear but it doesn't and instead becomes increasingly thick. This grabs your attention. Your brain moves you from a passive state to full and focused attention.

The absentminded way in which we often get from place to place, including everyday driving habits, needs to take a back seat in a new situation. A whole new set of skills comes into play as your brain seeks problem-solving strategies and your body tenses. Your attention gets laser focused on the task at hand—driving safely.

Picture this: as visual cues diminish you can barely see five feet in any direction. Your gaze sharpens. Your pulse quickens. Without the familiar markers you slow down and try to rely on instinct, experience, and other senses besides the visual—a most critical ability in navigating a car. You may not be able to stop as there could be vehicles behind you. The shoulder is no longer clear so pulling over may not be an option. Tension mounts. What to do?

This is where judgment and experience comes into play. You might lower the car windows and use nearby sounds as markers the way dolphins and submarines use sonar to detect the distance of nearby objects. Not hearing any cars gaining on you, you might slow down still more. You quickly calculate the various strategies and outcomes available to you.

Your entire driving history comes into play as you search for similar events from the past to provide guidance. In the meantime, your heart is beating more rapidly and you are so attuned to the moment that the typical daydreaming and list-making-while-driving activities disappear.

This experience mimics the loss of control typical of ambiguous situations when you travel in unfamiliar places where recognizable cues are absent, vague or misleading. Like driving in a fog, navigating yourself in novel situations requires a different kind of attention. Self-reliance and flexibility are critical to find solutions from your internal repertoire of stored capabilities. Fortunately, your brain and gut are hard at work. It's often surprising and reassuring what we can create when the possibilities seem slim. What would you do?

You call upon internal resources that you may not even know you have. What an exhilarating feeling when you succeed! Mastering the unfamiliar makes a journey more memorable, in a positive way. We really do have a vast number of life-experience combinations. We usually don't need to draw on them. It's so nice to trust that you can.

Though not usually as extreme as the previous example, travel generally helps us tap into the strengths and resources buried deep within us as a guide when the usual habits fail. In fact, one of the joys of traveling is tuning in to that deep inward source of wisdom, that part which is most awake and aware, perfect for the unfamiliar journeys through life.

Developing tolerance for ambiguity is one of the valuable byproducts of travel adventures. If you put yourself in situations that require openness to new experiences, you'll find that your self-reliance, self-support, and flexibility increases.

Adventure can be local. Distance from home base doesn't preclude novel experience. Anything that challenges your own personal limits will work just fine.

Here's an example from my own life. I live 40 miles from San Francisco and generally drive my car to get there. Though I spent my growing-up years in New York City where public transportation can take you almost anywhere within a couple of blocks of your destination, I'm unfamiliar with rapid transit in San Francisco.

My goal was to get to a known destination but in a novel way. I chose the train system known as BART, but it doesn't extend to a location near me. It would require a car to take me to the line's southern terminal, or I could take a different railway called CAL train, and then transfer at the BART terminal.

This would be a new experience because it's most comfortable to do what's familiar. Anything else requires more planning, strategic thought and sometimes discomfort. It was a work-in-progress until I began writing this book and thought about the benefits of reaching outside of my secure box. Yes, I knew I could get lost, exit in the wrong place, seem stupid to fellow travelers, and feel uneasy. But when I arrived, the feeling of mastery was worth it all!

Not a big deal you think? But for me it was. I did it and I was as proud as any four-year-old who managed to crayon a masterpiece without help. It wasn't perfect but I did arrive in the right place at sort of the right time. What limits your travel adventure?

Note any limitations below:

_____

_____

_____

_____

_____

_____

_____

_____

_____

Shut down your back-home mindset: Don't leave your head in San Francisco when your body is in Santorini

It's not easy to turn off a busy mind and stay present in a travel destination once you arrive. The process of getting away can feel rushed or chaotic or unsettling. You might wonder whether you remembered to turn off the lights, lock the door and manage a dozen different essentials.

Departures tend to be unnerving and these feelings can linger as your mind continues to replay the list of unfinished tasks left behind. You might be able to transition gradually on your journey to the final destination—if it takes you days to get there.

On the other hand, disengaging from home may require conscious effort and intentionality. Otherwise, there you are, maybe in sunny Greece (see photo on page 29), while your back-home mindset keeps you stuck at your departure point or suspended somewhere between the two locations, enjoying neither fully.

Why does this happen? The human brain depends to a great extent on learning and experience to plan, predict and manage the present and future. Other animals rely more on instinct to guide them. People look backward to make sense of current and future situations. It's how we learn. But looking backward can interfere with staying present. Conscious disengagement from home needs to happen before we can immerse in the here-and-now at our destination.

Human judgment gets better and better as we get older because we can evoke a growing library full of memories and even make novel connections between them. This is a vast amount of information which can create a downside. Previous learning evokes thoughts and feelings that aren't necessarily relevant to your trip. Better to leave them at home. But how can we separate these out?

You may need to manually shut down your back-home operating system (mindset) so that it doesn't interfere with the present experience. Here's how. Every time you find yourself thinking home-based thoughts, remind yourself to stop and substitute the present reality. It takes work but it beats missing out on your long awaited experience!

Here's an example. Let's say you left in a rush—a fair assumption. This tends to happen no matter how well planned the departure. Now your mind is running through a litany of unfinished tasks or worried thoughts about loose ends not secured—failure to stop the mail or the newspaper or a vague discomfort about a nameless something.

Cognitive-behavioral psychologists offer some strategies. They suggest that you imagine the worst consequence of forgetting to do something before leaving home. Now imagine the most positive outcome. The actual consequence will probably be somewhere in between. Can you live with that result? Continue to go down your list of worries, finding more realistic scenarios. Now let go of home entirely. When worry or even nostalgia creep in, repeat the process outlined above.

If you are a worrier by nature, or tend to have some anxiety that you usually manage by replaying and replaying troubling thoughts, you know how hard it is to trust letting go. I know this from my own personal experience—and it's hard to trust even expert guidance. But I promise you that if it works for me, which it does, you can do it too!

Let yourself be where your vacation travel actually takes place and savor the present. What would a Buddhist, Taoist, Yogi or Tai Chi master do?

Photo 7: Statue of seated Buddha

Spark wanderlust: travel vicariously

Travel through imagination has always been intriguing and one way to provide a time-out from everyday life—especially when actual travel isn't possible anytime soon. Since the invention of the printing press we've found ways to learn about the world through vicarious experiences—and travel the world without leaving home. Sometimes it's a choice, but it might be a necessity brought about by aversion to travel, lack of funds, or pressing demands at home.

Being creatures filled with curiosity about our surroundings and beyond, books in various forms like print, eBooks, audio books and stories transmitted orally offer a key to the unknown and exotic. It's a way to nibble at the boundaries of a new place without having to fully immerse, a chance to try out a way of life or an alter-ego without commitment.

The Odyssey, an ancient Greek tale widely read for centuries excited our ancestors about travel but also warned of lurking danger. Much later, *Gulliver's Travels*, written in the 1700's was an immediate success and since then has never been out of print. Curiosity about what lies beyond our personal experiences is a driving force in human nature.

Imagine being engrossed in a tale that seems so real that you can feel the thrill, or the pain, of the protagonist. Or maybe the story serves to whet your appetite for a similar real-life encounter. Books with compelling storylines keep us focused, entertained and fully immersed. More than that, by trying on someone else's adventure we can learn more about ourselves.

Some of my favorite reads do just that. Here are some suggestions: *The Artist's Way: A Spiritual Path to Higher Creativity*, gives precise instructions for seeing the world creatively and actually helps you inhabit the artist's life. As *Inward Travelers* we benefit by discovering our creative self, long buried or previously unknown in order to enhance and intensify travels in our own neighborhood or far-away places.

The bestseller, *Eat, Pray, Love*, takes you through the author's transformational quest for self understanding through Italy, India, and Bali. Searching for her place in the world, this book guides readers through an emotional process of finding oneself by immersion in unfamiliar cultures. The places provide background to the author's internal struggles and eventual triumphs.

Recent award winning *Down to the Sea in Ships*, chronicles the author's journeys as a passenger on giant ocean-going container vessels that bring consumer products to working ports in exotic places. It evokes life onboard and the real challenges of sailors and the unpredictable seas. It's hardly the day to day life you'll find on a cruise ship, but you might encounter some of it on a freighter that carries just a few passengers and travels to small and mysterious places.

Whether you read non-fiction, or fiction that takes place in a fascinating place, you can begin to fine-tune your own preferences for geography and culture long before you take your first step into a journey. Here's one from my own experience.

I read *Mary Queen of Scots* and very much wanted to retrace some of her steps in Scotland. When I finally made it to Edinburgh, Scotland I felt at home even though I'd never been there before. Because of my personal introduction through the book I was well acquainted with the tumultuous history of Scotland during the 1500's. It's descriptions actually helped navigate my sight-seeing. More importantly, history came alive as I imagined the drama of that long-ago time and place in its true setting. Walking the cobblestone lanes next to stone buildings that still have soot marks from the past brought to mind the coal fires that warmed early inhabitants in this northern climate.

Here are ways to further intensify your own sensations while you remain cozy in your favorite chair. Channel the authors' first hand thoughts, feelings, observations and experiences:

- Start with an author you love. For travel themed novels, James Michener is masterful. His extensive research on places make destinations come alive. Consider Michener's books about Hawaii, The Iberian Peninsula, ancient Rome and Chesapeake Bay, in America's south-east. Of course, he always included maps and timelines to trace the journey more precisely.

- Start with a place. Interested in India? Consider books written by Jhumpa Lahiri who makes her birthplace seem intensely real and jump off the printed page.

- Start with a biography of an historical figure who transformed his/her nation. It can give you an in-depth look at a place you'd like to know more intimately. Consider *Alexander Hamilton*, the book by Ron Chernow or the stage play his writing inspired. It provides a portrait of life in the British West Indies as well as the U.S. eastern seaboard in the late 1700s, as well as an in depth picture of colonial and revolutionary New York City and Philadelphia. It also gives you insight into the fledgling, often chaotic, United States government.

Armchair exploring avoids all of the hassles of the real thing, and it's one more way to satisfy your wanderlust.

Getting there and back: consider the possibilities

A journey doesn't simply begin at a destination and end when you depart for home. Getting there and back is a key part of the experience. How we make our way is integral, not just a logistics problem. And we often have more choices than we consider.

If an excursion is local, what's your first thought about how to get there? If you live in a big city it might be mass transit. Otherwise you might think car travel, but don't stop there. Could you walk, bike, or take an indirect but scenic route by bus?

Recently, on a trip to New York City, I decided to visit *The Cloisters*, a museum at the upper tip of the city that bears more resemblance to a rural setting in a forest of trees—with no high-rises in sight. In fact, the scene could easily be mistaken for medieval Europe which is what the museum's appearance intends and mimics.

The museum's website describes it this way: "High atop a hill in northern Manhattan's Fort Tryon Park, overlooking the Hudson River, The Cloisters museum and gardens is the branch of The Metropolitan Museum of Art devoted to medieval art and architecture. Featuring 5,000 works of art, including magnificent sculpture, illuminated manuscripts, stained glass, and the celebrated Unicorn Tapestries. Explore beautifully re-created plant, flower, and herb gardens of the Middle Ages."

I'd always wanted to visit *The Cloisters*, having grown up and gone to college in New York City, but it took over fifty years to finally get there. Having a tourist's mindset in a place where you were raised tends to take a back seat to the busyness of everyday life.

After an enthralling and magical day spent as if the clock had been turned back four-hundred years, my husband and I emerged from time-warp and faced the reality of getting back to central Manhattan, about 20 minutes away by subway. But we decided to take a much different route—slow, meandering, and above ground—the local bus.

Most of the time twenty-first century people hurry, even while on vacation, as if efficiency in getting to and from is always a benefit. But the journey back from *The Cloisters* was part of our experience. The slow bus stopped on almost every corner, giving my husband, who isn't a native New Yorker, a chance to people-and-place-watch for the two hours it took to crawl through crowded streets.

It was as if we were New Yorkers, even for a brief period, immersed in the daily life of the locals. We could feel the pace and mood which made it seem very real. Other bus passengers came and went lugging their bags filled with groceries and other items. I'd forgotten that most New Yorkers don't shop by car, but carry their purchases on public transportation. We alone took the route in its entirety just because we could. New Yorkers don't use local buses to sight-see!

Changing the transportation mode changes everything. When you drive, the number one priority, by necessity, narrows your focus. Maybe you'll see something interesting, but that's unlikely unless it stands out enough to shift your attention from driving. And that's probably not a good idea.

Walking allows you to get up close and personal with anything of interest that you see, hear, smell or touch. It helps to create a mindset before your journey that embraces openness to all experience encountered along the way. As with meditation, it requires you to notice when your thoughts distract you from staying present and to shift them back without judgment. Walking also gives you independence. You can veer off a straight line, go up a different, maybe more interesting street, and make discoveries not possible via other forms of transportation.

But some local destinations may be too far to walk. Then you might consider biking or busing. Both take more effort than walking and the first requires some skill and stamina. Both allow a shift in what you notice. For one, you are elevated from walking so your physical viewpoint is altered, changing *how* you notice. In many cities around the world rental bikes, electric bikes and scooters are available. These can be parked almost anywhere and left for the next person.

Of course, there are some places that are inaccessible or so distant that they require plane, boat or train to get there. And sometimes making the choice isn't necessitated by expedience, time or even cost—but rather curiosity. Consider some possibilities.

My own travels, for example, bring to mind a spectacular arrival in the Norwegian fjords by ship. A fjord is a long narrow and deep inlet caused by a glacier. It is one way that large ships enter Norway. The experience of arriving at the Norwegian coast via a fjord is tremendously satisfying but vastly different than flying into Bergen Norway or taking the railway from Oslo.

Entering the fjords midsummer on a ship before sunrise, the remaining weak rays of the sun were still visible in the night sky, while mists enveloped the horizon. As the ship moved into the deep water channel between the numerous islands, it was as if a surreal world had risen from the sea. The coastlines began to appear on both sides and were covered with summer cottages in bright colors. Small boats tethered to their individual docks bobbed in the water like rocking horses.

This was a dreamlike experience, evoking mythical comparisons to the bogs of Celtic England so beautifully described by Marion Zimmer Bradley in her 1983 book, *The Mists of Avalon*. It's been years since that trip, but I clearly remember the scene unfolding and still have nostalgia and awe remembering the splendor of Norway.

Next time you plan an adventure, spend a bit more time considering the *how* in addition to the *where* your journey takes you. Getting there and back might just be the most memorable part of your experience!

Photo 8: Numerous islands on the approach to Oslo, Norway by ship

Bring a journey home: the tangible and intangible

Tangible objects can keep memories alive. That's often why we buy souvenirs when we travel. These serve as reminders that cue our experiences and revitalize them as time goes by. But are things really necessary? I sorted this out for myself when I took a high-speed train from the port city of Kobe to Kyoto, Japan.

Tea ceremonies are hypnotic. I learned to appreciate the way these ballet-like performances unfold when I visited Kyoto. With graceful gestures, unhurried and choreographed like dance, geisha trained and costumed women acted out an ancient ritual. Time melted away in the slow motion process. That is the magic of the experience, charming and exotic.

Immersion in this experience requires a suspension of fast-lane thinking and feeling. Impatient and time-obsessed Westerners, yearn for newness and heightened awareness but tend to have trouble letting go. That was me: drawn to the elegance and significance of sharing tea while at the same time hesitant to relax into it fully because it required a shift from my familiar and comfortable frantic pace.

The rhythm of a tea ceremony is palpable, contagious and soothing— and definitely isn't compatible with cell phone or text-checking or extraneous stimulation that distracts. It requires suspending control of all that's familiar—so difficult for the contemporary traveler.

Let's say I could allow my breathing to slow and stay focused. Let's say I could actually relax into the moment and notice the attention paid to details. Then I could appreciate: silent, graceful tea-cup placement, tea infusion in water at exactly the right temperature, costume and sensual body language of the hostesses. I might notice cues that govern when and how to finally taste, if not drink, the tea. Then I could feel the sensation of a cup, warm to my lips, releasing a fragrant smell. I could feel warm liquid touching my tongue, gliding down my esophagus and disappearing from awareness. I finally gave in and let go, stopped analyzing, and melted into this ageless custom.

Soaking in the moment and enjoying the counter-balance to the noise in my head and home environment, I vowed to incorporate a semblance of the tea ceremony when I returned stateside. I imagined, and could even picture, re-creating this experience to lend some harmony to my typically stressed lifestyle. To this end I planned to buy a tea set, including a few small, intricately designed porcelain cups, the appropriate tea, as well as a few unfamiliar tools to create an authentic experience. Envisioning the perfect spot to capture the tea ceremony at home, I gave in to my impulse and purchased the trappings.

But can you really bring home a tea ceremony? The physical manifestation of a trip, the memory or even the emotions don't always translate sufficiently. Re-creating an event that belongs to another time and place may not be possible. Yes, there are the reminders that cue pleasant memories. But while I had good intentions, re-enactment means suspending some realities that are harder to shove aside. I gently tucked my tea ceremony accoutrements into the space I created in my cupboard but sadly never duplicated the experience.

In the end I realized that my travel, and maybe yours as well, creates an altered reality that permits and encourages seeing things with fresh eyes. Capturing and transplanting experiences may not be the point or even a possibility. Rather, the goal might be to take in and fully appreciate what is, and then let it go—until the next time.

The Japanese tea ceremony existed in that magical moment and may still be kept alive through memory just fine. For me at least, I recognized that bringing the tangible symbols home wasn't necessary.

How might it be different for you? List what's important for you:

_____

_____

_____

_____

_____

_____

_____

_____

_____

What to share with others: what to cherish for yourself

Some experiences can be translated and shared for others' enjoyment. Some defy language. Other thoughts and feelings seem too intimate, or sacred, or time-bound to make sense beyond yourself. The following story sorts the options.

I was standing by the ocean under a darkened sky in a remote place distant from any cities. The only visible light was from the stars overhead but when I looked up, the sight of so many twinkling objects was staggering—so much variety in size, color, and movement. The vastness of the universe, in contrast to my infinitesimally small self, triggered deep primordial emotions and shivers ran down my spine.

From the beginning of time our species has seen much the same scene in the night sky. And while I felt the experience deeply, there's no way I could describe it without losing most of its essence. That experience I'll keep to myself! What will you cherish but not share? There's no need to decide in advance but some things just don't lend themselves to telling.

Before the tan fades, or the hiking blisters heal, you may try to find words to describe your recent journey. Summing up, like in a photo show or travelogue, provides a shortcut to capture the memories. But the glorious moment-to-moment observations, sounds, smells, sights, interactions and self-talk that filled your moments might not translate into words.

How can you possibly share the myriad of memories with others in the detail and depth that was your experience? How can you conceivably capture its essence in the retelling? And why do you need to?

My recollection of the night sky is real and meaningful—even without communicating it to others. Choosing what and when to share is your decision, but you might want to think about why you pick certain events or perceptions and not others to recount. Since you can never re-live the happening through the telling of it, consider your goal in sharing. Is it to inform, as in giving a mini-lecture about something of value you've learned? Is it to create more intimacy by sharing your innermost feelings? Is it to prove to yourself or others how worthy you are? Is it meant to impress, to show how smart, well traveled, courageous, intelligent or even wealthy you are?

Some experiences are easier to describe in words than others. You can depict a scene, explain a conversation, or describe an event using language, photos, illustrations or memorabilia from your travels. If you can express yourself through an art form like painting, photography, writing, cooking or music, you might try to communicate the memories symbolically. Without words you are left with emotions, sensations and gut reactions that are generally harder to label and often more deeply felt.

Watching the sky from a beach on a clear, dark and starry night may evoke sensations of timelessness and agelessness. At that moment you might feel transported back to the first human's observation of the universe—full of wonder about its vastness or its purpose. That transcendent flash belongs to you in a way that its telling might actually fail to capture. You'll know it when it happens. Then preserve it for yourself.

If you leave your ego aside, as well as your need to prove yourself, what then merits communicating and what might be treasured by yourself, for yourself? Sorting this out doesn't need to be a scientific process. Make it more intuitive.

What to share with others and what to cherish for yourself is not a simple formula but rather a complex set of options—exercised at a journey's end. The *Inward Traveler* looks inside for guidance in making a decision that's more intuitive than logical—a mix of emotions, self-knowledge and the unique adventure. Honor your own perceptions.

Trusting Your Senses:

Introduction

We are born with the capabilities to perceive and experience life as physical bodies that depend on sight, hearing, smell, touch and taste, as well as what some of us call a sixth sense, intuition. Our five senses are hardwired in the oldest part of the human brain which may be why we take them for granted—until they don't work as they were designed to do. When your vision changes or hearing diminishes you take notice.

Even with the extraordinary vision that most of us are fortunate to have, we often don't see the whole picture. The same is true for the other senses, also underutilized. While the neurological mechanisms may work just fine, what we actually see, hear, feel, smell and taste requires focused attention to register in our conscious mind. But in today's world, focus is in short supply.

This section explores the senses in action. It also offers ways to boost creative expression by supercharging the senses, while also sharpening the experience of life in general. *Flow* results from focus and optimal attention—whether at home or half way around the world.

Magic: Just Outside the Kitchen Window

Steam rose from the fence and mingled with water droplets as they fell from overhead tree limbs and leaves, lime green in the early spring. Sun rays pushed through the foliage yielding super-saturated colors, almost too bright for the early morning.

I didn't go far to discover this drama playing right in front of my eyes. It happened just outside of my kitchen window, a magnificent show that I easily could have missed. Sitting at my usual counter stool peering east through the window, I'm reminded of the *Inward Traveler's* mantra: "It's the journey, not the destination." So much beauty right there and available for an observant viewer.

I stayed with the quiet experience, amazed at the intensity of a green or red leaf, wet from the rain but illuminated by the sun. I saw the whole scene, literally, in a new light knowing it wouldn't last long before a slight rotation of the earth changes the scene. I tried to drink it all in.

A drop of water hung from a leaf with sunlight and a breeze causing it to shimmer like a diamond. There might've been a rainbow nearby but I was so mesmerized by the current scene I didn't move. I'd captured a one-of-a-kind masterpiece of physical beauty that might never appear exactly the same way again.

Nature presents matchless artwork, and you don't have to go far to see it, to capture it visually or symbolically. While I'm certain that a similar scenario was available to see during the twenty-five years I've peered out this same window drinking my morning coffee, it was unique today simply because I stopped to notice.

Then the sun shifted its attention and the magical moment was no more. Still, I retained the memory which inspired me to express it in some way. How that happens depends on how I use my creativity.

If I were a visual artist, or comfortable sketching, I would try to grasp the splendor—the reds, greens, browns and the gem-like drops of water that linger after the rain. I would take my pastels, charcoal, water colors or oils and try to preserve their essence, my feelings, and the moment.

Photo 9: Outside the kitchen window, the shimmer of wet greenery

If I were a composer or musician, I might be inspired to set the scene to music. But if I felt blocked in ways to communicate about it or show something tangible. I could doodle, or dance or sing or bake a pie! As a writer, I'm doing what I can to deepen my pleasure and remember the moment to re-experience at a later time.

The scene outside my kitchen window will never repeat itself exactly, but like a kaleidoscope it offers almost infinite variations for visually stimulating my senses, if and when I am ready. And in the meantime I can search for new ways to express what I just saw.

How might you respond to such a commonplace, and yet extraordinary, scene, that sparked your sense of wonder at the very moment your brain registered it?

_____

_____

_____

_____

What would you do to celebrate the moment?

_____

_____

_____

_____

Frame your experience: seeing through the camera's lens

Take a look at a sensational scene in your backyard or half way around the world and then photograph what you see. Let some time pass and then retrieve the picture. Take a look at the picture. Which details did you miss seeing with your own eyes when you first snapped the shot? What did the camera capture without your conscious intention?

Your brain and emotions beg you to remember images that seem awesome and noteworthy. Preserving them in your awareness ensures enjoyment over and over again. But you may not want to trust your memory to recall the details.

A camera lens mimics the eye and captures the visual image your brain identifies. Being a physical object, the camera records what is actually present. Ironically, it can record much more than what you're actually paying attention to as you snap the picture. So you may wind up getting additional features or even less than you bargained for.

You may want to capture a scene, live action, a person, an object, or a color. In thinking about your creation you focus narrowly on replicating precisely what you had in mind. This includes as many aspects as possible of what your eyes saw, at that very moment in time. And so you carefully frame and click; or maybe you hurry to capture live action—something ready to bolt, flee, fly.

Here's an example. Imagine that you take a hike in the mountains during early fall. Visualize a palate of deeply colored leaves that flood your senses. Notice the trees shedding chocolate hued bark, uncovering their pale under-skins. The sun's filtered light warms the space between the trees and casts a sparkle on the swaying greenery.

Late season foliage and berries hang from the trees like Christmas ornaments. Then you look at the photo and it's not what you remember seeing.

The camera takes in and records only what it is capable of recording—everything physically present but not necessarily your intentions. If you are disappointed when you look at the resulting photo, consider doing it with what the Buddhists call a *beginner's mind*, as described earlier—a childlike curiosity that's unbiased and un-opinionated. See what's actually there, not just the slice of time and space you envisioned at the time you took the picture. Perhaps your camera saw something remarkable that you didn't. I found that out first-hand.

A memorable scene comes to mind from my own experience. Some jagged rocks jut out of the ocean offshore in Shell Beach California, a small non-touristy town adjacent to its famous cousin, Pismo Beach. The quiet, beach-bungalow framed community has a lovely, quiet and peaceful oceanfront park with few visitors. I chose to sit on a bench right there overlooking the scene which my husband's camera lens captured in a pleasing way. What I mean is that I liked the way *I* looked—something that seems to happen less and less as I age!

Weeks later I pulled up the image to find it a possible home in my online album. What I remembered turned out to be much less interesting than what I actually saw in the snapshot. Yes, the lens captured my likeness at that place and time but so much more. My wind swept hair reminded me of the vigorous coastal gusts that made it almost impossible to keep my sun-hat on my head. The paper cup in my hand brought to mind the independent small-town coffee shop where I found a custom brew to-go along with a chatty server interested in where I was coming from and headed to. The photo also evoked the pleasant drive up the coastal highway from Los Angeles to San Francisco on my birthday. It gave me a chance to be grateful for my good fortune and health in what is now my old age.

Using a beginner's mind, what do you now see that you didn't notice when you shot a particular image in the first place? The camera freezes everything and displays only the moment the picture was taken, so you now have the opportunity to spend as much time as you want to review that moment. Remember, you're not looking for anything in particular in the picture. Rather you are becoming aware of things that the camera saw but didn't register in your conscious mind.

Whether you now see something amazing or quite ordinary is not the point of this exercise. Rather it's a reminder that what we choose to focus on is what we see and remember. The rest escapes our attention. Our brains cannot take everything in, to process and preserve as memory. But it doesn't mean that what is at the periphery or beyond our notice is less interesting.

Metaphorically, the point is to occasionally de-focus and just see what's there, to purposely look beyond foreground. You can do this quite well with what the camera captures, and/or you can take the time to let more of life in by, metaphorically, broadening your frame.

Capture the moment: intentional noticing

Some yellow wildflowers caught my eye while walking a familiar trail in early spring. These first flowers signaled new beginnings, rebirth, energy and the coming of warm weather and longer days. I might have seen the flowers in my own garden, but looking and noticing is harder to do at home with familiar cues, distractions and endless lists of things to be done. So I planned a day trip.

Photo 10: Wildflowers in early spring

"Going away" even for a few hours enabled me to focus on a moment in time captured in a color-washed meadow with nothing to get between my experience and me. There is so much visual stimulation in our daily lives that it's easy to disregard much of what is plainly in front of us to avoid being overwhelmed by too much information. Noticing and seeing has more to do with intentional focus than with functioning of the visual cortex. Day to day we tend to concentrate on the business at hand, whatever it is, and any extraneous information tends to get set aside unnoticed. Ironically, this actually has some evolutionary advantages.

In the days of our ancient ancestors, taking time to see and smell the wildflowers could cost you your life. Survival was the name of the game and unless the wildflowers had some crucial medicinal or nutritional benefit, better to stay vigilant for cues about a hungry predatory animal lurking nearby.

We are programmed to notice first and foremost what will keep us alive, even though the daily dangers we now face are far less critical. Still, the pleasant more relaxed behaviors that make us feel good and slow down our breathing, signaling peace and safety, get only crumbs of attention. Our lengthy, never ending priority lists feel urgent and demand attention before what may be perceived as frivolous—seeing the beauty around you.

It's really impossible to see wildflowers, even when they're right under your nose if your mind is occupied with demands that don't include seasonal change. If you're multi-tasking or attending to what's pressing, you risk missing much that connects you to your spirit, the natural world, and pleasures that are abundantly available without a cost. That's why setting time aside to fully focus on what is plainly there in front of your eyes is both possible and refreshing emotionally and physiologically.

Seeing through someone else's eyes, what might otherwise seem irrelevant to you, allows a somewhat different perspective. Taking a walk with a dog or a child, whose visual field is much closer to the ground, might help you notice something curious, like an iridescent ladybug, or a fuzzy caterpillar clinging upside down to a leaf.

Walking with a birdwatcher or gardener will direct your focus in other novel ways, toward visual cues that you'd probably never notice on your own. Those chance encounters may provide new connections between ideas or thoughts, open your mind in a fresh way, or solve a creative problem. Maybe the water color you're working on needs another element, or the story you're writing needs a description that's eluded you until now. A fresh viewpoint does the trick.

Even something as simple as turning to the right at the street corner, rather than to the left, can lead to a visual surprise. Time of day, time of year, current weather, all influence what and how we can see things. You might walk when you feel blocked in your ability to produce a creative result or simply take a walk for inspiration.

Excluding the same old visual distractions can make new associations easier to form and surface into consciousness. Many of the world's most famous scientists and artists pushed through creative blocks while taking a stroll. Maybe this is a good time to get out those walking shoes!

Smell: Activating our most primitive sense

Animals depend heavily on their highly developed smell to shape their experiences and memories, powerfully guiding their behavior throughout life. Not so much for humans even though the olfactory sense, the most primitive of our five senses, produces recollections that are incredibly powerful.

Smell and taste are some human senses that are intense in children but lose power over the course of growing up. As adults we rely heavily on complex and abstract ways of understanding the world and communicating, sometimes even losing track of our most basic instincts, like smell and taste. But sensitivity to smell and taste can be rekindled.

Can you recall or re-live your time in a place where smell was front and center? As I write these words I'm remembering the yeasty smell of pretzel shaped bread wafting from a tiny bakery on a plaza in a small town on the banks of the Rhine river in central Germany. I've forgotten much about Miltenberg but not the aroma of dough baking.

My nose guides me back to the place. Not only can I still see myself eating the traditionally shaped pretzel on a stone bench outside the shop on a cobblestoned walkway, but I see pigeons strutting nearby impatiently waiting for crumbs. I see local families dressed heavily for the late autumn cold laughing while they nibble on still warm morsels.

Another olfactory memory, but from my early childhood, offers a cue. I can still conjure up the smell of freshly baked bread in my grandmother's apartment. That recollection brings back the warmth of my grandma. Her kitchen was the center of her world, and mine when I was with her. Baking was the main language of our communication. Breads and pastries were our handiworks. Though she spoke mostly Russian, which I never understood, we worked together seamlessly. The smells we produced are my most profound, positive, and lasting olfactory memories.

Many years later a visit to Turkey inspired another powerful memory centered around smell: a tea ritual. Just a sip of apple tea rekindles memories of the enormous spice market in Istanbul. Whenever I raise a certain gold-rimmed Turkish demitasse cup to my lips I get a hearty whiff of spiced apple tea. It arouses many olfactory memories which reawaken my travel experience.

The tradition steeped Istanbul bazaar, as big as ten football stadiums, remains a highlight from my Turkish travels. I can still see myself wandering through the isles of brightly colored and pungent seasonings in this timeless gathering spot. It's been there since the middle ages when the spice trade first linked east and west in serious trade. Women shrouded in burkas or colorful head scarves loudly negotiated prices with vendors wearing turbans and mustaches who later called out witty phrases in heavily accented English or Turkish to attract new shoppers' attention.

I remember bins of caramel-colored curry powder, yellow saffron, black anise that caught my eye from a distance but up close it was always the smell. Separate and blended, a medley of exotic aromas awakened my senses, and now I feel the pleasure of associated memories from the bouquet of spiced tea.

Photo 11: Istanbul, bazaar spice market

Do you have olfactory memories? Are some of them linked to travel like my experiences in Istanbul? We so thoroughly depend on visual processing that it's easy to disregard the other four senses, or even additional ways of recognizing experiences. We accommodate to smell all too quickly, which means that after sniffing a strong scent like perfume or even rotting food or the nearby sewer, we don't notice it after a few minutes. When that happens it's easy to stop noticing other less intense smells, missing out on some fascinating olfactory experiences. It doesn't have to be this way.

How can you use your savoring of scents and aromas to create pleasure or enhance creative expression through writing, painting or music at this very moment?

- Take some time to do a backward glance at smell-focused experiences like picking berries in the woods or baking chocolate chip cookies with mom.
- Build a smell adventure into your next trip: maybe the fish market in any seaport town or the vanilla scent when you scratch the trunk of a Jeffrey pine tree in the forest.

The sound of silence: deliberate disengagement

Have you ever gone someplace to listen to the silence? I wasn't looking for that when I ascended a mountain-top overlooking the majestic Waimea Canyon, the "Grand Canyon" of Hawaii. At that moment there was total quiet. Almost 5000 feet below I could see but not hear the white water of ocean waves crashing on the shore. It was an eerie feeling to hear only the sound of my breath or the ground below my feet as I hiked the dirt path. Even the chirping of birds and the scurrying of land critters were absent at this altitude.

Photo 12: Overlooking the ocean at Kalalau Lookout, near Waimea Canyon, Kauai

Escaping from all external noise is getting harder and harder to do. Finding a place away from cell phone service and the incessant electronic sounds of current life requires planning. And apparently that's a practice that's uncomfortable for many of us. Recent psychological research confirmed that silence is so unpleasant for some people that they would rather self-administer electric shocks as an alternative to staying with their own thoughts while deprived of other stimulation and sound.

In one rather extreme study, participants were left alone in a room for 15 minutes without books, electronic devices or paper and pencil. 67% of the men and 25% of the women self-inflicted electric shocks to avoid the absence of external stimulation. The takeaway was that some people don't know how to steer their thoughts in a pleasant and calming direction so they try to avoid being alone with themselves.

As a society, we are so accustomed to hearing external prompts that, when absent, fear tends to get triggered. Learn to embrace the quiet, let your thoughts and breathing come to the forefront of your attention, knowing that there is no real danger in doing so. This allows more potential for awareness, growth, and peacefulness, which are hard to retrieve in other ways. You can learn to embrace the silence or understand why you distract yourself from it. The *Inward Traveler's* path meanders through the world of the senses as well as the world of experiences. Both lead to a fuller, richer life and enriched creative process.

Rick Hanson, Ph.D., author of *Buddha's Brain: The Practical Neuroscience of Happiness, Love and Wisdom* wrote about taking pleasure from our senses. According to him, paying attention to certain sounds can intensify pleasure. He suggests the sound of "waves on the seashore . . . and silence itself." But I wouldn't begin with silence as the past few paragraphs suggest its difficulty.

Take the time and notice the quiet. Relax into it. Let your observations and internal chatter come and go, catch yourself going on a tangent with some thought or feeling. Choose to let it go, and stop if and when it seems too difficult or unnerving. Return to the silence when you can.

As I basked in the quiet of the mountain top I wondered how else to find this blissful state when the experience of the moment faded into a distant memory. It could be as simple as taking a time-out from electronic chatter—no phones, computers, TV, radio, and for the moment no sounds of people or animals begging for attention.

Sometimes my noise-cancelling head phones do the trick. Designed for air travel, I sometimes put them over my ears to block sound instead of listening to music or talk. I simply relax into the gentle white sound of nothing. Ten minutes will do. And then I'm transported back in memory to that awesome, hushed, peaceful mountain top.

Body language skills: fine-tune the unspoken dialogue

Stranded at the foot of Mt. Fuji, Japan, I spent an amazing afternoon in the small town of Shimizu after being rained out of my first plan. In spite of its looming presence, the mountain was engulfed in fog which made it invisible. Getting an up-close encounter with this majestic peak, which was the goal for that day, just got crossed off the list of Japan's highlights not to be missed.

The reality of travel requires back-up strategies which brought us to a non-touristy shopping center on Shimizu's main street. The local vendors benefitted from the rain that diverted other would-be mountain gazers to their cobblestoned mall—outdoors but mostly covered.

Midway down the street a kimono shop displayed their wares on the walkway. A team of women wearing kimonos beckoned passersby to stop and experience a free fitting. Maybe a regular occurrence, but possibly it was staged for the benefit of other stranded tourists and its bottom-line potential.

With nothing pressing or more interesting to do, I stopped and looked at the traditional silk gowns saturated with color—peachy orange, crimson red, deeply hued turquoise. I had no intention of shedding my warm raincoat and other outer clothes to publicly don a kimono. But in fact, that's what happened.

Totally without language, since the local women spoke not a word of English, we negotiated the process—everything from agreeing to the fitting, selecting the colors I would prefer for my kimono, and mutual understanding that there was no charge or purchase expectations.

Two petite Japanese women, standing less than six inches from my body, worked front and back, applying many layers of foundation, scarfs and bustles which they chose for me in response to a wordless nod. I could feel their breath and touch, see their eyes close to mine, all of this intimacy based on mutual consent of some sort. Careful to not look directly at them, I showed signs of appreciation by bowing and smiling. We created a rhythm and it worked.

Wherever you go, new encounters with people give you practice at fine-tuning your skill in understanding their ways. Even without language there are certain universals like smiling, frowning and disgust. From our earliest days we've learned to interpret others' behavior by watching their expressions. Our survival often depended on that. Even babies can detect anger and pleasure by watching and then reacting accordingly.

We provide impressions to the onlooker, from head to toe, based on how we appear and move. These communications don't require language, but precisely because of that they are prone to misreading, especially when the other person has a different cultural origin or language.

The *Inward Traveler* takes a mindful approach to learning. Ideally, before a trip take time to acquaint yourself with local customs, it provides a bit of a foundation. But real-time, in-person watching is always the starting point. Closely observe how people greet each other, use gestures, carry their bodies, determine physical distance within and across genders and ages. How do they relate to children, relatives vs. strangers? Is the style of the host culture formal or informal? Is the country predominantly the same ethnic, racial group,

Photo 13: Kimono fitting on a rainy day in Shimizu, Japan

or more diverse? At first, simply register what you see and notice how it affects you—how it matches or conflicts with your own history.

Silently but not passively, continue to observe, see and feel. But stay aware of the natural tendency to judge, to categorize and interpret situations because that's how our brains work to make sense of things. Just as in meditating, (section 1 in this book) the goal is to stay present, breathe, notice what is actually taking place rather than getting sidetracked by other thoughts or hunches or stereotypes.

In the American culture we tend to be more self-focused than other-focused and our tendency to worry about what others think about us can interfere with taking in what we observe in others. Note that tendency and gently shift back to observing when necessary.

The accidental stopover in Shimizu became a cherished memory of my travels through Japan. Feeling my way through a novel and somewhat strange encounter left me feeling tremendously pleased and sensing a closeness with two women who were no longer strangers to me. Never mind that it lasted no more than an hour.

Shifting Perspectives: mindfulness in action

Introduction

Travel takes us to places near and far, but it also broadens our ways of experiencing the world of ideas, feelings and assumptions. Travel can shake up pre-conceived notions about ourselves, others and the planet we inhabit. This section explores the *Inward Traveler's* capacity to grow, change behaviors, and continue to evolve while exploring the internal and external world mindfully. Eight mini-chapters show you how.

How travel augments therapy: leaving the couch
behind

Once while alone in Paris I did something uncharacteristic that
allowed me to work on my shyness. Arriving solo at a restaurant one
evening, the maître d' asked if I would like to sit alone or join another
single person. Such an idea back home would have made my spine
shiver and my heart race uncomfortably. But in Paris it didn't seem so
unusual. I took the risk and joined a man about my age, 37 at the time.

My dinner companion spoke little English and I, no French. We both
spoke a little Spanish and laughed a lot. My lifelong habit of avoiding
unfamiliar and uncomfortable social situations, received a jolt. Years
in therapy hadn't budged this discomfort, but taking a risk in Paris
opened a new door to change—still a work in progress.

In the hey-day of Sigmund Freud's practice in Vienna, he cautioned
his patients about traveling—which meant straying too far from the
analytic couch in his office. Back then, many of his patients consulted
the good doctor as many as five times a week for talk-therapy. The
commonly held belief was that therapy needed to be the central focus
of life. Most of Dr. Freud's patients were wealthy women with time
on their hands and concerns that now seem mostly archaic.

In today's world, travel while working on one's own internal
processes, no longer seems unusual. There may actually be some
hidden benefits to traveling, whether by choice or necessity, while in
therapy. Times have changed. Few among us would choose the rigor
and demands of daily therapy, nor is it financially feasible.

Therapy and supportive counseling, unlike analysis, provide tools for
processing our concerns with a professional who provides a different

perspective and / or a comforting outlook, typically an hour per week, sometimes more or less. With space between sessions there is time for self-reflection and practicing new behaviors.

Over time, therapeutic styles have evolved, broadened, and democratized, giving more of us access to professional psychological support. Creative therapists with flexible approaches can tailor support, whether scheduled once a week, once a month or even via email or FaceTime. The goal is to incorporate therapeutic activities into our lives rather than build a life around going to therapy.

However, since learning can be slow when the external environment remains unchanged, travel can facilitate change. Consider some undesirable habits like lighting up a cigarette outside your back door following dinner, or arguing with your spouse about how to load the dishwasher. Familiar cues can trigger unpleasant emotions like anger, fear, and sadness. Highly reinforced patterns are hard to break.

When you are traveling, if you are also concurrently in therapy, you're already primed for attending to your thoughts, feelings and reactions. You may even know what triggers your unhealthy responses even though they are difficult to change. Travel can speed up the process.

The *Inward Traveler's* journey highlights internal experience. Meandering through the physical world with your eyes, ears, and mind fully alert, challenges you to take in the often overlooked obvious as well as the subtle. Changing the environment, which results in new external cues, might help change how you respond. Breakthroughs in self-understanding follow more rapidly.

When you are away from home, at work, or engaged in any other daily activities, there's an opportunity to build new patterns, reinforce new connections and generally observe with fresh eyes.

For example:

- Follow a cup of coffee with a walk instead of what you typically do next.
- If you watch TV before going to sleep, try taking a long bath or shower instead.
- Try out new and healthy but uncomfortable behaviors that you might not attempt at home. Stretching oneself can lead to a state of *flow*.[2]

Perhaps there won't be a dishwasher to hassle with in your travels, thereby avoiding an argument in the first place.

Build new habits to break the link between the familiar, highly practiced cues at home, and the knee-jerk and habitual reactions that seem automatic and unhealthy. Take a trip to encourage new learning and facilitate new patterns.

---

[2] Experienced as intense concentration that can block worry or anything not relevant. The sense of time can become distorted and self-consciousness disappears, replaced by a feeling of well being.

Travel as therapy: shift your mindset wherever you go

All living things have the built-in capacity to move away from pain and suffering toward repair and wholeness. Trees find a way to grow into the light and away from darkness. Humans seek relief from physical or emotional hurt also. Some of us travel to try out new behaviors or to get away from old ineffective or detrimental patterns. We have many options.

Seeking therapy is just one way. Therapy's benefits include feeling happier, more self aware, more comfortable in relationships, more compassionate or better understood, to name a few. But a journey of any kind can also serve as a conduit for emotional relief, recovery and new growth.

Therapeutic travel can take you far away or work just as effectively close to home. A meditative walk, while not what we usually think of as travel, might help clear a troubled mind and suspend judgments, self-criticism, and non-productive worry (meaning worrying about something over which you have no control). While it's not a permanent solution you might get some rest and an opportunity to look at things differently. Even a brief time-out from worrying has therapeutic benefits like slowing your pulse and momentarily shifting your attention.

Nature is therapeutic, soothing, and plentiful even in big cities. In the midst of the busy and fast paced city of Hong Kong, I found a peaceful park that seemed to have been stopped in time. Here was old China, with red lacquered pagodas and formal, traditional gardens. I took a time-out there to gather my thoughts and take a rest from sightseeing.

Photo 14: Peaceful retreat in the midst of bustling Hong Kong

Parks are everywhere and the trees they house come in all shapes and sizes from very petite and shrub-like to the giant redwoods of northern California.

Metaphorically, a tree is a nurturing mother offering comfort— offering a resting place, providing shade, sometimes fruit, and always a reminder of a life force that's steady, sturdy, and yet ever changing. In fact, we humans share a great deal of a tree's DNA. Unlike most other living organisms, trees are especially long lived. Ancient redwoods have presided over the forests for more than 2 thousand years. Okay. They beat us by a long shot!

There's a California Live Oak along the route of a trail I enjoy walking. What makes it special is her strange formation. She tolerates my weight very well with just the slightest movement that resonates with me like a mother cradling a small child—which is how I feel in her embrace.

Photo 15: Tree as comforting mother on a trail, Stanford, CA

The leaves gently rattle above and seem like music—the tree's comforting voice. I feel safe and restored. This is nature as therapy; this is a tree as loving mother. You don't need to travel far to find one!

Traveling to distant or unfamiliar places gives us a chance to create new, more adaptive patterns. A fresh venue provides opportunities for practicing a new way to think about something or react to it. You might try keeping a daily journal, initiating conversations with total strangers, or solving unfamiliar problems in getting around. Keep in mind that in the background of wherever life takes you there's a strong and embracing tree on which to lean, waiting patiently. In her shadow you can relax, sit, notice, and—write in your journal.

Therapeutic travel can also be a metaphor for shifting a mindset rather than simply embarking on a trip. That's what Ann learned. She usually spent major holidays with her extended family but that became less frequent as time went by. It left her feeling uncomfortable and adrift without a plan for an upcoming Thanksgiving. Holiday time can be particularly upsetting if your model is the idealized commercial version portraying family togetherness. Think of media ads touting holiday celebrations.

Dreading the approaching holiday season, Ann worried about the void and how to fill it. Fueled by anxiety she pushed herself to create a few alternatives. Not knowing how to decide between them she flipped a coin and chose to volunteer at a local soup kitchen. This satisfied her need for contact with people and a meaningful way to spend time. Giving herself some new options down-shifted her anxiety to positive anticipation and enhanced her mood. The dread of holidays subsided a bit.

It's well known that repeating the same thoughts and behaviors in the same context produces the same results. A journey of any kind shakes up the context and allows you to create new links to new outcomes. The context in Ann's case was the new environment—a soup kitchen, full of unexpected, novel experiences and encounters requiring new tactics and new actions. It launched a new and healthy tradition initiated simply by the flip of a coin!

Travel, whether around the corner or around the world, has potentially therapeutic benefits. The feeling of mastery is a powerful tonic.

Quiet yourself: downshifting the gears

If it were possible to notice your daily frenetic pace in real time you might be able to catch it when it peaks. Then you might be able to consciously throttle back tension and restore equilibrium. Imagine that in this process you could also upsurge your creative juices. The *Inward Traveler* values this kind of awareness—but real and imagined barriers often block the path.

Our lives are so complex and continuously bombarded by stimulation of all sorts. You have your own list but here's mine at the moment. New emails announce their presence on my laptop, and bills wait patiently on my desk begging for attention out of the corner of my eye. An auditory reminder on my online calendar cues a dentist appointment in 30 minutes. A loud knock on the door, then the sound of a truck pulling away, indicates that a package was left. I just can't let it sit outside—it might disappear.

I reach for my coffee cup, but the contents taste cold. Now I need to warm it in the microwave which means walking 100 steps from my office at the back of the house to the kitchen where I'm sure to get further distracted. My head is swimming with jobs that all seem pressing. Can I squeeze everything into 20 minutes and refocus on my writing—my primary goal only a few minutes ago? My pulse quickens as if there's real danger, but only the dentist appointment is a fixed commitment.

Though it's possible to get better and better at multitasking, there's a point beyond which our effectiveness decreases and stress increases. No matter what our age, doing more than two things at once results in poorer performance. It's a fact. Unfortunately, most of us don't notice that shift as we push forward, as if checking the boxes on to-do lists is what life is all about. Control and mastery of our responsibilities provides so much gratification that it's easy not to see the downside.

Try an experiment. Make a minimal commitment, let's say ten minutes, to restore equilibrium. De-escalate, unwind and return to the present moment—the only point in time that really exists. Use a time-out to catch your breath and focus your attention. It's almost as essential as breathing—according to science (based on stress management research).

Here's an example of how that might work. Set you clock, smart phone or a different device to ping you several times a day—you decide when. Pick times when an interruption won't derail something essential. Give yourself some options for using the ten minutes. Maybe play soothing music and slow down your breathing. Maybe listen to sounds of nature like rain, ocean waves, wind, birds chirping.

Close your eyes and imagine being safely transported to the place where the sound is coming from. Don't be limited to listening. Perhaps you can find a texture that feels good to your hands and stroke it for a while. A furry, silky or other tactile surface works well. It might bring out your baby-self stroking a blanket or "lovey." Do this with your eyes closed.

What other brief restorative strategies might you currently use? Look out the window? Stop and get something to drink? Take a bathroom break? If these actions come to mind, you're already tuned into your body/psyche's needs. Journaling, meditation and mother nature all aid in quieting yourself.

Journaling, just writing with no particular goal, gives you the freedom to let your mind wander on paper or online. It helps downshift your gears to idle. What you write is not the point, nor is grammar, punctuation, or spelling. Taking the moment to record your present thoughts, feelings and observations is all that's essential. And it needn't take more than ten minutes; less than the typical coffee break, especially if that entails a trip to the neighborhood brew house.

Similarly, meditation provides a time-out to notice your breathing, or listen to your heartbeat, or experience the sensation of cool air entering your nostrils. Whether sitting, standing or walking, focusing on your breathing is the vehicle to inner quiet.

Noticing nature in any form—even a good screensaver with colorful tropical fish, a mountain scene, or the beach you sat on last summer, takes even less effort. But it also means suspending any thoughts that carry your attention away. For example, you notice the tree outside your window that's just beginning to bud. This is a good start until it reminds you that it's time to start mowing again. Stay with the tree and redirect any other thoughts back to it when your mind strays. A few minutes is all that's required for these quick restorative time-outs.

When you find a strategy that helps quiet the internal and external noise, it's yours for keeps, wherever life takes you.

Positive psychology: enjoying yourself is a state of mind

At this very moment the morning light filters through the ten foot shrubs outside of my office window and the breeze catches the leaves. Their movement creates a dance of light and color. When I take the time to notice I'm comforted by the tranquility. Taking the time to notice is the key.

Whatever the activity, look for joy in the commonplace. Maybe it's the walk in your neighborhood, taking the commuter train to work, a pleasant memory, the absence of pain in your body, or the lingering taste of your morning coffee or tea. Yes, there is much that is wrong in the world, but teach your attention to find its opposite whenever you catch yourself dwelling on a downer.

It's easy to focus on what's wrong, out of place, imperfect or lacking. In fact, it seems to be hard wired in us, stemming back to humans' earliest experiences with survival. Over the eons we've become experts in keeping an eye out for what could go wrong, or recalling what did go wrong as a way of avoiding catastrophe. This was an adaptive skill that still has some usefulness today.

But our concern for what's negative can easily block what's right, good and pleasant. Keeping positive thoughts and emotions in mind is a challenge well worth the effort. But it won't happen by itself since negative tinged experiences seem to stick in our memories easily while positive ones tend to simply slide away. That's the way the brain evolved.

No two travelers to the same place, even at the same time, share the same experience. Personal demographics like your age, where you're from, your cultural background and stage in life all play a role in your inner-travel experience as you explore the outer world. But even when people are compared, and matched on the above traits, what I might call the "positivity" factor can lead to different ways of observing a journey and recalling it later.

If you have a constant stream of negative or fearful thoughts and feelings just below the surface of awareness, you are not alone. Evolution has made some of us so adept at spinning these bits of pessimism we hardly notice. Periodically, try to notice a negative thought and interject a competing one: hopefulness, gratitude, or pleasure. No need to make it up. Just look around for something to appreciate, even something small that you might otherwise overlook—like, the traffic on your commute was light today!

Opportunities for celebrating the *good* surround us. At this moment a Bach suite plays through my computer as background music while I write. Most of the time I don't hear it, distracted by whatever else is top-of-mind. But now, as I consciously choose to listen, I'm swept away by its beauty and infused with a moment of positivity. I need to do that more often and also spend some effort recalling the enchanting sounds I just heard—it will stick better in my memory that way. Remember, if it's more difficult to retrieve and hold on to what's good, you can thank or blame your evolutionary history.

But taking a positive stance leads to feeling happier, which enhances mood and can even normalize blood pressure. The research on happiness strongly endorses the efforts required to increase your happiness quotient. Independent of your personality style, family history and inborn temperament, happiness can be learned. It is one of the few qualities humans can enhance through practice.

The ability to find the positive and celebrate it is universally available. Gather these moments in your memory, as you have them, and recall them later. It's a well researched therapeutic strategy for managing depression. And it's available to you immediately by looking for something that delights your senses in the space that surrounds you right now.

Maybe it's a photo of a loved one? Maybe it's the birthday card sitting on the table next to you from a dear friend? Maybe it's the bird perched in the tree outside your window? Maybe it's the lingering taste of a warm or cold brew you just swallowed? Opportunities for enjoyment are everywhere. You just need to pick them out of the internal and external clutter.

Be here now: manage your attention

Traveling near or far allows us to disengage and unplug, and maybe shake off some preconceived notions about the things we see, hear or feel. But rather than appreciating real-time events as they are, it's all too easy to stray from the present moment to some other time. This happened when I saw the round-topped and hazy mountains in Guilin, China from a ship on the Li River.

Represented in Chinese paintings that go back hundreds of years, these mountains seemed familiar to me. I remember seeing copies on the walls of the the Chinese restaurant in my childhood neighborhood. Even then I was struck by the grey, misty, and majestically curved figures rising out of the water like saucers standing on edge. You'd think that when I actually saw them for real I'd be awed and spellbound. But I found myself comparing them to other mountain ranges I'd seen. I was off somewhere else and totally missed a highlight right before my eyes.

While our stream of consciousness is always busy arranging observations, thoughts and feelings into categories, we don't have to slavishly go along for the ride. Focusing attention on *now*, needs to be a conscious choice. My observing self noticed that I'd strayed from what I came to see and dragged me forward to the present moment.

The days to come are unknowable and unpredictable. That's the nature of the future. Even when the past and future seem bleak, *now* can hold meaning and pleasure. Stay with the present: today, this week, this month—the only time that is available for experiencing anything.

Today might be a good time to get away, even if it's just for a sliver of time. Can you spare an hour this very day? If so, remember to start with an optimistic attitude for your experience. What's good about today? What works just the way it is? What are you grateful for right now? What do you currently appreciate? What pleases you or any of your five senses? At this very moment, why are you glad to be alive? If you catch yourself thinking "yes, but ..." you've strayed from your experience. Gently guide yourself back to *now*, this precise moment.

One day with a couple of hours to spare, I took a hike and set my intention on *noticing* rock formations that often serve as background scenery, a frame, but usually not the focus of attention on their own. Observing in a different way and picking a novel viewpoint can change your experience. It changed what I paid attention to, and the ways in which I saw them.

The boulders and outcroppings seemed arranged as if to please a photographer or painter's eye. It surprised me. While it wasn't a show-stopper like Stonehenge, the formations had their own charm in several shades of earth tones, turning to gold with the sun's warmth. Wild flowers and grasses peeked out of the shaded crevices. I wondered how randomness could yield such delight.

Photo 16: Boulders and outcroppings with wildflowers.

It's easy to get sidetracked from the present. A stray thought, image, or sensation can surface in awareness and entirely sidetrack your goal.

The Buddhists refer to this as *monkey mind*[3] at work. Get distracted by a shiny object that triggers a memory—and you're caught in a web of stories and far away from your body's experience. And so it was with me.

---

[3] A Buddhist term meaning restless, unsettled, and capricious

Trying to shift my attention back to hiking and the rock formations that were supposedly my focus, I found myself instead thinking about Stonehenge and Druid rituals. I had once again conjured up thoughts that took me away from the present. While tangentially related, given the culture that surrounds some of the world's most intriguing man made constructions, I was on a mind-tangent and not on the same path as my feet.

I nudged my attention back to the rocks lining the path. While minerals served as my objective for the day's walk, birds or ground squirrels would have been fine subjects. Simply noticing my breathing would have been a perfectly acceptable objective also.

Next time you're out and about, make a conscious choice to focus *your* attention on a new aspect of a familiar situation. When your focus shifts, simply catch it and guide it back. For the *Inward Traveler,* the journey matters more than the destination, to paraphrase Confucius.

Increase life's intensity: compress time

If you could condense everything that matters to you into one day what would be important to emphasize? Compressing time is a way to clarify what's really essential and special in life. The goal of this exercise is to optimize meaning and pleasure while greatly narrowing the time frame. How would you live such a day?

Though it might sound morbid at first glance, focus your experience on this day as if it were the last in your life. Ideally free of other demands, this could be accomplished most easily when your daily structure is minimal—perhaps on an unscheduled vacation day.

If you can't actually get away, dedicate an at-home day when you can freely follow your passion, and dedicate it to the following question. What path would you take if today were the last day of your life? How would this day be spent? Create some time urgency to explore what's most important.

Being human is both a blessing and a curse when it comes to understanding mortality and the finiteness of our lives. We have the capacity to understand the impermanence of everything including ourselves, unlike most other living species. Yet we live, for the most part, as if we had all the time in the world until our permanence feels threatened.

Having a near brush with death because of accident or illness, or the loss of someone close, reminds us that life circumstances can change in an eye blink. At that moment we want to know that our choices for living are meaningful and satisfying. Why wait for a catastrophe to experience such moments? Here's a chance to try on some ideas.

Start by imagining a very desirable and gratifying meal. Plan it. Choose and then see the ideal ingredients in your mind's eye. Picture how they're combined. Envision the whole process, and then view the final presentation as you've designed it in your awareness. But don't limit yourself to the first dinner your imagination conjures up. Consider other pleasing food scenarios and let these come together with a picture of the meal as its ready to be served. Enjoy your creation!

Now instead of a meal, imagine your last day of life with all of the ingredients that will make it memorable. Does it include elements such as people, projects, emotions, a trip down memory lane? Let the vision become even more vibrant by including specific people, perhaps, and envisioning how to share this moment with them. Or leave people out, if that's your preference.

Are there projects so important to you that you're willing to take your last day to work on them? What are these commitments? How would you prioritize them and why? What emotions get evoked, and how do you acknowledge and pay respect to them? If memory lane is your choice, what stands out as essential in a backward glance at your life?

Take this day to clarify priorities, to see opportunities for change or adventure or consolidation of ideas and relationships. Come away with a fuller understanding of what really matters and what is merely window dressing. Keep what's essential from this experience as a gentle cue for maximizing each day's significance. Live the life that matters to you—this day and every day.

My intention is not to be morose, but can you imagine your own obituary and what's been written about you? How might it be different than what you might have written about yourself? Is there a way to bring these disparate pictures of yourself in alignment? This is a practice to align and sharpen some internal pictures of who you are and ways to polish and refine that persona.

As I sit in my backyard contemplating these very thoughts, some birds chatter and brown tree squirrels climb the giant umbrella shaped native oak tree dangling acorns like holiday ornaments. The air is warm and still, which lets me hear a Shubert piano piece coming through the speaker of my computer. The early autumn light is soft. My garden, weeds and all, contribute to my sense of calmness and tranquility. I am at peace. My thoughts briefly shift to all that will remain undone, unsaid. I take a breath and dismiss that reflection. This would make a good last day!

Follow your curiosity: novelty and creativity

If our very distant ancestors hadn't followed an adventuresome path the human race might still reside only in the African grasslands. Travel feeds our curiosity. And if travel to far off places appeals to you, it may be because of this inborn inquisitiveness.

Hunters and gatherers of long ago followed the food wherever it took them and our tendency to look beyond the familiar remains to this day. We descended from wanderers for whom home meant only a safe place for family and tribe with enough food and water. Only much later did people settle down in one place. But the urge to see over the horizon is as strong as ever.

Curiosity is a human trait but not everyone chooses to travel. Self-described home-bodies need to satisfy their wonder in different ways. If big travel via plane, train or ship doesn't appeal, enjoyment might come from shaking up a daily routine or environment. The comfort of sameness, paradoxically, can lead to boredom.

Finding freshness in everyday life requires only a change in perception, in what you focus on. Leave your home, don't go far, but do something uncharacteristic. New ways of seeing the same scene actually shakes up the sameness of repetition.

You can start by locking your front door with your non-dominant hand. Then, instead of looking straight ahead in the direction you usually go, look to the right and left, look down at the ground or gaze up toward the sky—with your naked eye or a telescope. Notice anything interesting? Do any novel thoughts or associations surface?

Head for the nearest patch of flowers, weeds, a tree, shrub, rock cluster or other miracle of nature. Spend a minute looking at whatever your eyes land on and see what sensations or observations surface. What do you see that you didn't notice before? Touch its surface. Note its texture and temperature. Bring a magnifying glass next time. Get close up the way a two-year-old might. Any interesting insects nestled into crevices?

Extend this practice to a five-mile radius. Identify some nearby place of interest and enjoy visiting there until monotony sets in. Then challenge the status-quo by visiting the very same location at a different time of day or season or branching out with someplace similar. You might consider a nearby garden where seasonal transformations seem magical. This may satisfy your curiosity and hard-wired, primordial yearning for novelty—without going far.

Take an alternative route on a favorite walk. Choose a new café or grocery to heighten the awareness of drinking coffee or choosing vegetables. Drive instead of bike or the other way around. Pick a different day of the week or time to run routine errands. What do you observe?

It may sound minor but changing even a small detail can positively alter a habit or make something quite routine feel exciting. And you don't need to stray very far from home. Henry David Thoreau, a 19th century naturalist and philosopher lived in his cabin at Walden Pond in Massachusetts for two years noticing minute changes in the environment—even the tiniest daily progression of a flower bud was a cause for his wonder and joy. According to Thoreau, "It's not what you look at that matters, it's what you see."

Empathy: a walk in others' shoes

Traveling answers so many questions about what pleases us—what resonates with who we are. But what we see, do, and think about can be ego driven. Though our own experience is a logical starting point, the frame might be limited by long held beliefs or stereotypes. Immerse yourself in the culture of your destination. It can broaden your perspective and appreciation for the host country and its people.

Once, while vacationing in Turkey, I stayed at an inn in central Istanbul which was originally a stately home. Its architectural details represented long-ago Moorish design with intensely colored and intricate geometric tiles.

The physical beauty of the place was reward enough. But at 5 AM the first morning, a surprising event occurred that filled me with deep and lasting appreciation for Muslim traditions—an unexpected happenstance that's happily a byproduct of travel.

Chanting in Arabic from loud speakers not far from my opened window woke me from a deep sleep. I realized that this was the first call to prayer of the day, in a country steeped in Islamic customs. Drawn to the window, I was mesmerized by the chanting which brought chills and goose bumps to my skin. Mind you, this is not my tradition, but I found it emotionally evocative and powerful nevertheless.

Photo 17: Early morning chanting, heard from the nearby mosque

Looking out into a courtyard where I could view windows of nearby apartments, I observed people unrolling prayer rugs, as is their habit. The whole experience helped me realize how integral the five-time daily call-to-prayer ritual is to the life of the locals, orienting and anchoring their days. I'd never thought about this before, but have done so many times since then.

First-hand experiencing of the traditions or history of a place can provide a snapshot of life of the locals at that very moment, or even at another point in time. Having what psychologists call an "as if" experience can deepen and intensify feelings, allowing you to identify with those who lived there and then. It's a wonderful opportunity for increasing empathy, the ability to put yourself in someone else's shoes and have their experiences vicariously. There's an added benefit: breaking down some walls that feed ignorance, stereotypes, and preconceived notions.

Expand your understanding as you notice your own values and how they mesh with, or are different from, the culture of the destination. Face-to-face encounters can reduce xenophobia, the fear of strangers that often leads to intolerance. It lets us identify with people in new ways.

A good friend of mine provides a related story about his trip to the Coliseum in Rome. Standing in that historic place, he imagined that he was coming face to face with a lion, as was the fate of prisoners and slaves long ago either for punishment or entertainment of spectators.

He'd never thought about it before but being there evoked intense feelings of fear and disgust. Retreating to the viewing-stands in this virtual experience, he found it difficult to empathize with the onlookers' blood lust. Still he understood that the spectacle had some political and social value in its day. He came away shaken but with a deepened understanding of himself and his place in history.

Similarly, another friend described her travel to Dachau. It was the first Nazi concentration camp to serve as a model for subsequent death camps. Walking through the concrete and barbed wire enclosures, feeling the chill of death and horror surrounding her, she imagined what it might have been like to be a prisoner there—bringing chills and tears to her eyes—and a profound awareness of the horrors and inhumanity that existed at that time and in that place. She silently vowed that she would never let this happen again—if one person had the power to make a difference.

Not all travel serves solely to entertain. According to the experts, happiness doesn't depend on just pleasure or gratification but on taking a path that satisfies our quest for meaning. Sometimes the meaning derived from our experience enhances our humanity and increases our compassion—which of course makes us improved and more powerful versions of ourselves.

In the end, our ability to feel others' suffering enriches and expands our capacity to understand the complexity of life.

Photo 18: Natural beauty brings pleasure to the viewer, anywhere

Managing Risk and Change: spin a positive scenario

Introduction

When life throws us challenges, we need to find ways to work around them. Coping with the unexpected and unwanted can be a daunting test, unless you are a daring or danger-seeking soul. In the following section you'll discover some ways to approach on-the-road situations that seem difficult physically, psychologically, emotionally, or spiritually. Find out how to manage them. Test your moxie and your ability to adapt. Learn to overcome obstacles in healthy ways.

Flow[4] is activated when you stretch into your discomfort. The task may take all of your concentration and you may find yourself so immersed in learning or understanding whatever you need to do, that time fades away, stands still or, conversely, passes in a flash. Your experience can be exhilarating, exciting, and totally engaging. Your body may tingle as all of your senses intensify in response to the test.

---

[4] Review definition of *flow* on page 27

Adventure or risk? Ocean kayaking:

To facilitate daily living, we humans tend to be creatures of habit. Day-to-day life leans toward predictable for most of us. Introducing new schemes voluntarily into jam packed days has low probability of happening. But, under favorable circumstances, we might free ourselves from the constraints that usually apply.

With the right set of ingredients, we might allow ourselves more latitude to explore, to notice, to consciously choose new options. That's why it's much easier to try uncharacteristic adventures while on vacation. Without the predictable cues that pervade our daily lives, we can more easily suspend the same old responses and be more open to engaging in new and novel behavior. I learned that firsthand quite by accident.

Though kayaking isn't exactly high-risk behavior or an extreme sport, I tried ocean kayaking for the first time, in my seventies, in Hawaii. Here's how a never-considered experience can happen with little trepidation, especially away from home.

Down on the beach at Hanalei Bay in Kauai Hawaii, a handful of kayaks lined the sand in front of the old wooden pier. I noticed some youngsters, maybe seven or eight years old, diving from the far end. What a way for local kids to spend a week-day in summer! Judging from their skill and tanned bodies, I guessed that they were regulars. I marveled at their playfulness and swimming ability at least thirty feet out from the beach—totally comfortable, like a pod of baby dolphins.

Photo 19: Pier at Hanalei Bay, Kauai, Hawaii

Then my attention shifted to the kayak lesson about to begin and the mostly awkward looking learners, seemingly tourists like me, probably not seasoned kayakers. The scene registered in my mind and gut as a project that just might be doable. I came away feeling a bit courageous and even excited at the prospects of trying on a kayak experience.

It had never occurred to me before, and still might not have, but for that accidental walk on the beach at Hanalei Bay that morning and stumbling on the scene of some kayaks sitting straight up in the sand like arrows waiting for their orders to ship out. And I got hooked.

It's not my style to throw caution to the wind, but away from the usual restraints and responsibilities of home-life and fixed patterns of thinking, I impulsively signed up for some lessons. Afterwards, and before the next day when the lessons were scheduled to start, the rashness of my decision created doubts and fear. But not wanting to forego my deposit, I took the plunge.

Here's how the story unfolds and ends: Hours spent in the ocean, managing the paddle and riding the white water waves, gave me an adrenaline-charged, exhausting, exciting, and totally satisfying way to spend time. I don't know whether I'll ever do it again, but that's not the point. I challenged the limiting self-perceptions I held about my own capabilities and had a magical time!

If you are young, which is a relative term, you have an advantage here. But if you are middle aged or beyond, keep in mind that many of us tend to become less and less adventuresome as we age in terms of trying new things.

Our palates and stomachs tend to prefer what's familiar so exotic foods are generally less appealing. The same can be said for the activities we engage in. Still, regardless of age, traveling can be the key to suspending what's safe and comfortable. It allows you to keep pushing the limits and age restraints as you explore the world *mindfully*.

What new out-of-the-box experiences did you have on your last vacation or would you like to try? How about a "zip-line" in Costa Rica, a trail ride by horse on a dude ranch, a spin on a motorcycle or motor scooter, a drive in an ATV vehicle in the desert, or guided cave exploration? Can you imagine bringing your experience home and incorporating some part of it into your everyday lifestyle? Here are some ways to proceed:

- Notice how many of your pleasurable activities seldom happen;
- Identify a pleasurable activity associated with a past trip—real or imaginary;
- Determine if an equivalent is available where you live;
- Find time, at least once, for this activity.

Did your experiment result in good feelings?

_____

_____

_____

_____

If so, see how you can make it happen again.

_____

_____

_____

_____

If not, what else might you try?

_____

_____

_____

_____

Escape the beaten path: Wilderness travel

I'm on the bow of a ship that's passing through the Chilean fjords, surrounded on both sides by hills green with lichen, moss, and small shrubs but little else. Even at the end of summer the peaks are dusted with snow and clouds that obscure the tops of some crests hang heavy with moisture.

The stark beauty of landscapes untouched by civilization is staggering. If ever there were humans or other animals present here, they were careful to cover their tracks. The picture in front of me can't be easily captured with a camera, as on these generally overcast days there is little visual contrast between the ocean, the sky and the mountains.

This place is splendor reduced to its most basic elements and appeals to the most primitive aspects of our human nature. Though civilization has encroached on most physical settings, the Chilean fjords remain a primordial landscape. With evolutionary ties to more primitive life forms in the past, some of us humans still crave the simplicity of life at its most pristine—a throwback to eons past.

Fantasies and longings aside, the fjords are not the kind of place where getting lost in nature would ever be your goal. This landscape is not hospitable. Magnificent to view from a distance, I was relieved to think about the Chilean fjords poetically from the safety of a large ship.

If you need a taste of the majesty of snow covered mountains flowing into ice fields to satisfy your *Inward Traveler*, you might be able to have such an experience but it does require some people planning. Though the austere beauty of the place is a given, the companions you choose to share this with should be compatible with your needs for space or quiet or wonder. Otherwise you might want to consider a solo wilderness trek.

You can have a time-out from twenty-first century living and perhaps a once-in-a-lifetime challenge at no extra cost. You can choose to live, even briefly, in the rough, natural world of our distant ancestors for whom it was routine—but I don't recommend a layover in the Chilean fjords!

What if you need time alone to think about a loss, a new beginning, an ending, or another life transition? Maybe you want to prove your hardiness to yourself. Whatever the reason, if the wild calls to you and you can make it happen, try to follow your instinct.

Cheryl Strayed, the author of the best selling book, *Wild*, did just that— escaping a life that appeared to dead-end in a painful place. At the same time, she was also grieving the loss of her mother, the one stable figure spanning her twenty-two years. She took an extreme action to jump start a new life.

In an excerpt from her book she looks back on her journey and makes this observation: "And then there was the real live truly doing it. The staying and doing it, in spite of everything. In spite of the bears and the rattlesnakes and the scat of the mountain lions I never saw; the blisters and scabs and scrapes and lacerations. The exhaustion and the deprivation; the cold and the heat; the monotony and the pain; the thirst and the hunger; the glory and the ghosts that haunted me as I hiked eleven hundred miles from the Mojave Desert to the state of Washington by myself."

The author's extraordinary months long hike on the Pacific Crest Trail spanning coastal California and Oregon proved her resilience, endurance, determination and sheer will to re-invent herself. Strayed's difficult history began to recede into the past, and she owned her new strength which gave her courage to move on in new and healthier ways. *Wild* chronicles her amazing encounters.

I don't recommend that you follow in her footsteps as she was scarcely prepared. But if wilderness travel appeals to you, you might want to plan it better and start small. Try carrying a full backpack for a couple of miles first. Understand the conditioning your body needs prior to an extended hike and prepare for possible dangers—animal, human, natural, as well as long stretches of time alone.

But if you self-identify as extraverted (please see the chapter about introversion/extraversion in this book in the section: "Mind and Emotions at Work"), then be sure to plan your time and itinerary to meet up with other trekkers at pre-determined spots.

Assuming that this kind of travel appeals and becomes a serious interest, find a guide book that sketches major U.S. trails like the Pacific Crest in the West, or the Appalachian Trail from Georgia to Maine spanning 2,174 miles. Way too lengthy for most of us, you might find that segments lasting from 1-15 days better fit your time constraints and energy.

If solo wilderness travel is not for you, look for other adventures that take place in small groups like mountain climbing and safaris. Even a local adventure is satisfying if it has some risk. Maybe board a local bus with no map and no destination. Get off where you please to just explore. Taste the wild in your own way!

Start over: Try on a new you

Have you ever wished that you could go someplace new, become a different person, or at least try on a new personality or behavior? In our home environment everyone knows us based on our usual patterns—our typical ways of speaking, reacting, preferred lifestyle, and opinions. Our intimate acquaintances accept us to varying degrees as we are—sometimes for better, but maybe for worse.

Even when we try to change a typical way of doing things, or attempt to respond uncharacteristically, other people's expectations may actually inhibit change. Our attempts to shake up our repertoire may actually cause waves of discomfort—to us and them. Much of how we live and interact with people is patterned and predictable. When something changes, like a long held opinion or style of dress, or way of communicating, it gets attention.

Much of our daily interactions become automatic and therefore comfortable. Though not usually conscious, pushback from others or the setting we live in, tends to maintain *homeostasis*. This is a law of physics that applies equally well to human behavior, the tendency to revert to a comfortable, stable equilibrium.

But you can free yourself to change. It's easier to try on new variations of how we look or behave while away from home. Travel may be the just right intervention. In a new setting, the people you meet don't know the way you are "supposed to be." In whatever way you present yourself, that's the way they experience you. When you're free of familiar prompts, places, people, and other cues that typically influence your behavior, you have a chance to tweak an old pattern that you'd like to modify or discard.

Whether the change is significant or minor, trying it on for yourself, uninfluenced by your community, is a great starting point. Here's an example of a small and not too momentous change in my own life. My husband, who always wore a mustache since he could grow hair on his face, decided to see how it would be without one at age fifty-five. While waiting for his plane to depart for China some years ago, he went into the men's room in the airport lounge and shaved it off.

During the next three weeks he interacted with strangers who didn't have any opinion about how he *should* look. He got to try out his appearance and make his own decisions without focus on his face by family, friends and acquaintances who would sense something was different and probably comment about it—and maybe push back against the change. We're used to seeing people and our environment in a static and predictable way—again, the comfort of homeostasis.

When my husband returned home, he'd already decided that the change suited him and notwithstanding some of the reactions, especially our daughter's upset with dad's facial change, the modification became permanent.

Start your change process with small tweaks. These fit more easily into daily life. Then move on to behaviors that require more practice to make them stick. Here's an example of a more challenging type of self-change. Let's say that through feedback from others or your own self-awareness you see a habit that you'd like to change. Let's say that you tend to interrupt in conversations, or talk over others, or show impatience. You'd like to work on that.

It may annoy you that your tendency to talk is greater than your capacity to listen. In a new environment with strangers who see you solely as you present yourself and not based on your history with them, can you try to be a better listener? Keep in mind that this habit is quite difficult to change in a short time frame so it will work best if you have enough time to practice. An away-trip of a week or two is ideal but long before you leave, take time to visualize interactions in which you take a breath, or count to ten, rather than interrupt or jump into a conversation too often or too quickly.

When you feel ready, prompt new acquaintances with questions and remind yourself to listen to their responses intently. No need to perform or impress through talk, though it will be tempting. How does this feel? What did you learn?

Use the feedback, likely non-verbal and subtle, to further modify your style. Continue to try on variations until you feel comfortable and practiced enough to do the same when you get home.

Social Stretching: Travel to meet people

Travel is the perfect vehicle to practice your social and interpersonal skills, meet people from a certain culture, or immerse yourself in a culture different from your own. This kind of journey requires openness to new experience and the ability to tolerate the ambiguity that comes with spontaneous happenings. But first, here are some basics for approaching strangers and the first step in getting to know someone:

- Understand and become clear about your motivation: Are you simply practicing new behaviors, reinforcing recently acquired skills, or seeking a friend, companion, lover?

- Research your host culture: Determine whether communication between genders is OK, inappropriate or even taboo! How are men or women, alone or in pairs, perceived? Watch others and learn.

- Spot a person's receptivity from her/his body language: Are you seeing a red or green light? Does this individual seem open to contact? Is their attention focused toward the outer or inner world? Their facial expression—especially eyes and mouth—tell you a great deal. Their standing or seated body tells you still more. You don't need a psychology degree. Trust your instinct here.

- Make the most of chance encounters: Waiting in line, seated on trains, planes, or in cafes provide perfect opportunities. Again check out your neighbor's receptivity to making contact. Initiate a comment or even a glance. Their reaction will let you know whether a next step is in order. If yes, that's where small talk skills are beneficial.

- Small talk fundamentals: What's there to talk about with a stranger? It turns out that everything is possible. First find a common ground. The fact that both of you are in the same place at the same time provides a starting point. Maybe commiserate about some relevant frustration like waiting in a long line, or being stuck in an airline terminal, or on a slow train.

- Take a conversation to the next level: Try going deeper into a subject rather than superficially covering topic after topic. Gently probe for an expanded response. Ask your conversation counterpart if they want to say more about the topic or offer your own history or experience on the subject.

- Show your interest by asking questions: Be gentle and sensitive in your query. Look for body language that suggests the other party is uncomfortable and then back off. But people appreciate a good listener and you might learn something you didn't know.

Now here's what that means in practice: Quite by accident you might meet someone and in that moment whatever ways you use to initiate or respond to them determines whether you'll click. If you hit it off, you can get to the next step which might include a follow-up meeting. You then have a chance to present yourself in ways that may be novel for you—a chance to practice a new skill or behavior.

For example, you might decide to make warm eye contact and show uncharacteristic emotion, just to try out a part of your personality that you wish to expand. You might call it role playing but it's not really acting as if you were someone else. It's trying on less familiar and less developed parts of yourself.

Meeting a new person may allow your more outgoing side to flourish because your new acquaintance didn't know that you are the quiet type. Conversely, try on playfulness if you are the serious type. It will feel like a stretch but you'll learn something about how you feel displaying this more hidden part of yourself. Use your own feedback loop to fine tune. Ratchet up or down depending on how it goes. More humor, why not. Less talking, worth a try. Remember, you're *trying on* a role not *adopting* it. There's no downside.

When you're ready, consider venues that specifically foster meeting people. Traveling to meet people from a certain tradition, nationality or culture can be arranged through in-home stays. Aside from usually being an inexpensive way to travel, there's no better way to learn than by immersion into another person's life. Simply renting someone's extra room maybe with meals is one way to go.

Perhaps your goal is to learn Spanish through an immersion program, or learn to cook regional Italian food. You can get to know your hosts well and occasionally form lasting bonds. You can also learn how other people seek meaning, find joy, manage conflict or stress, as well as navigate daily occurrences.

Keep in mind that this form of travel can lead to an intensity or intimacy that feels one sided or uncomfortably close. But learning ways to regulate distance with other people to avoid anxiety is another useful skill, not beyond your grasp.

The threat of danger: successful coping

You never know about your own moxie until confronted with a new and fearful situation. It's only then, sweating and pressured to think quickly, that you test your nerve and judgment.

I saw my first coyote up close and personal—just ten feet away while walking my usual trail on the hills behind Stanford University. The rural outdoors is, after all, not a Disneyland set and belongs to the wilderness creatures that live there. Still, I'm a big city transplant, and it caught me by surprise.

While my cerebral cortex was trying to logically and reasonably predict my actions, my primitive instincts, often humorously referred to as *lizard brain*, kicked in. This mode of action is instinctive and controlled by the central nervous system. In a split second, my lizard brain sprang into action assessing the potential danger, and I tried to predict whether I would handle any actual encounter heroically or with panic.

Without conscious effort or thought, my focus narrowed, my heartbeat picked up, and I quickly scanned the nearby terrain for cues. I saw a ground squirrel perched on the limb of a nearby tree signaling in loud chirps to others of its kind that a predator lurked close-by. But being neither a rodent nor a cat, which are a coyote's preferred prey, I seemed not to be in imminent danger.

Some background information might be helpful here: Coyotes are slightly larger than dogs, but still in the dog family. At about 20 pounds they are like medium size collies, more likely to be afraid of you than vice versa. Unlike the wolf who avoids human contact, the coyote's range has extended in the wake of human civilization. It's not unusual for coyotes to reproduce in metropolitan areas, but it is unusual to see one on a hiking trail frequented by humans. Of course this information was not available to me until much later!

Along the trail I saw a couple of other hikers who must have assumed that they were seeing a dog, even though it's unusual to see a dog walking unleashed and without a human companion. A few folks were so engaged in conversation or engrossed in their electronic devices that they missed the event entirely. Their obliviousness didn't increase my sense of safety or provide reassurance. I was obviously on my own here. As for them, well, they were oblivious.

Photo 20: Coyote taking a hike

In the end, the coyote veered off the path and back into the deep brush. For as briefly as this event unfolded, my near encounter with the coyote was still quite an unnerving adventure! But I learned something about my coping abilities. First of all, I credited myself with paying attention and noticing. I appreciated my central nervous system response: alertness, rapid pulse, and scanning for danger and escape options. Also, without too much panic I was able to assess the danger and quickly identify possible strategies and outcomes.

When I spotted the coyote while hiking, I noticed that it kept a safe distance at about ten feet, curious but walking parallel. I saw that as positive, giving me time to assess the level of danger. If this animal wanted to charge, it could have.

I still had time. What could I do? I had a sweat shirt around my waist which couldn't do much to protect me, unless I swung it over my head in circles to give an impression of being a larger person, and therefore a less ideal target. So I did it. Swinging the sweatshirt made me feel better—that's also important in a tense situation—the feeling of personal power and control, entirely subjective but useful in managing panic.

I thought of all I knew or had read about the danger of running away from large animals, so I decided to stand my ground and, if necessary, back away slowly. I made eye contact and held my gaze as a way of communicating that I wasn't afraid. Good thing the coyote didn't get closer since an animal's sense of smell would have given away my fear!

And, finally, I measured my odds in a real showdown. I remembered the self defense class I took long ago and thought about how to protect my vital organs while at the same time injuring or chasing off the coyote. Remember that predators of all kinds are looking for easy prey. Thankfully, I never needed any of my strategies but neither did I feel helpless.

When you travel, whether around the globe or around the block, the unexpected can happen. Potential dangers and other unsettling events may occur, and you can't plan for these. Or can you? Learn some new strategies to cope with perceived danger and threatened loss of control. Anticipate some possible problems and visualize options. Be vigilant and don't be distracted by your smart device except where you feel totally safe. Human predators, maybe animals too, pounce when they think their prey is distracted.

There are some obvious caution markers. Consider the place itself, based on safety reports from the U.S. State Department, other embassies or a reliable news source, as well as the time of day. Note any facts about the travel destination that seem relevant. You can prepare in advance—sometimes by avoiding high risk options.

For example, it's not wise to ski in deserted areas alone, nor is it a good idea to travel as an unescorted woman in many places in the middle east. Also, keep in mind that a woman who gives a friendly smile to a man is considered flirting, or worse, in some Latin American countries. Prudent measures are easy to determine in advance and to plan around. But how do you cope with the unexpected, like a predator on the hiking trail, animal or perhaps human?

First, don't panic. Don't let your instinct (lizard brain) take over. While it will help you focus your attention and prepare for fight or flight, it doesn't use logic, or your past experience, or the executive function of your brain that lets you plan, even under intense pressure. Consider your options. Think about the tools at hand, including your own body—its mass and strength. Be inventive. Use your creativity to fashion a novel solution. And breathe!

When The Unanticipated Happens: choose how to respond

Travel enhances life. At least it should, but many unanticipated happenings can get in the way. How you handle them makes all the difference between enjoyment and disappointment.

If you are a planner and expect an orderly progression from one occasion to the next, know in advance that once you depart home base, and sometimes before, not much remains under your control. Travel is dynamic, and anything can go awry. But sometimes the deviation from plan can lead to an unexpected and remarkable adventure.

I was circumnavigating South America on a ship and after two days at sea the next planned port of call was the coastal town of Punta Arenas, Chile. But, as is often the case in the rugged very far-south Pacific, the winds blow ferociously at gale force. As the ship approached the dock, which wasn't exactly a sheltered harbor, we learned that it wouldn't be our safe haven in the storm.

The port had just been closed because of treacherous weather. The dock master feared that a ship as large as ours, could smash the dock quite easily leaving a splintery mess that would cost time and money to repair. From the standpoint of our captain, a precise German and low risk-taker, the integrity of our ship could be compromised by docking, leaving me with the image of the Titanic as it began to take on water. We soon received the official word—our ship planned to go off-course. But the sound of gusting winds and the ship's turbulence announced the situation well in advance.

On our trip around Cape Horn, we didn't get to one of the destinations promised in the glossy brochure from the cruise line. And it was easy to feel cheated. I tried to keep in mind that how I internalized this circumstance might well determine how I felt about the entire experience. I really had a choice—positive, negative or neutral. Could I remain curious and open to an adventure that might unfold in ways I couldn't foresee, without pre judgment? That's what I tried to do.

Instead of the impossible itinerary caused by an unexpected Antarctic storm, the captain set a course for Campo de Hielo, Patagónico Sur, a glacial field in the Southern Andes mountain range of South America, that we otherwise would have missed. Few travelers ever get to this ice flow, more than a day's journey away from our original destination, and off the beaten path for ocean liners. En-route we witnessed an immense rainbow spanning the entire Straits of Magellan, which is one of the most southern land masses in our watery world and devoid of all human habitation.

The relevance of the glacial field is that it's one of the last remaining in this part of the globe due to climate change. The sight made my skin tingle as I realized its scale. Using binoculars, I could see what looked like a toy boat and some ants moving about at the foot of the glacier as it began its slow-as-a snail's descent into the warming sea. You don't realize the enormity of this glittering blue/silver and melting mountain of ice until you observe that the ship in the distance is an ice breaker, and the ants are full sized humans exploring its base on foot.

Our ship hovered for nearly a day, enough time to enjoy this other-worldly scene, and the shifting colors of ice enhanced by the low sun that lingers in the sky almost all night during the southern hemisphere's summer months.

Photo 21: Melting glacier and ice field in Patagónico Sur, Chile

This side trip was an accidental outcome that I couldn't anticipate but wouldn't have wanted to miss. Change can be unnerving and upsetting, but there just might be unexpected or awe-inspiring rewards!

Part of the fun of travel is the positive anticipation associated with researching a new venue. Become thoroughly familiar with its nuances ahead of time. Virtually savoring a destination in advance heightens your senses, enhances your experience, and increases your pleasure upon arrival.

But disappointment is bound to happen when you're forced to abandon your well-made plan which, by the way, is not such an unusual occurrence as itineraries can change depending on weather or local factors at the blink of an eye. When that happens, serendipity can intervene and sometimes make things as good or even better.

Return to health: how travel planning gets you there

A close friend planned a trip to Paris. It was an extraordinarily important marker for her. It followed a year of recovery from a death-defying, life-changing illness.

During her recuperation, daydreaming and detailed organizing distracted and filled hours of discomfort. She confided that her lengthy hospitalization was tolerable mostly because she spent her days in reverie about the particulars of her wished-for trip. It added meaning and purpose to a low point in life. The anticipated pleasure-quotient attached to this upcoming experience kept her going, and helped maintain a positive mood.

While Paris may not be for everyone, this long awaited return visit provided her with in-the-moment good feelings and, according to neuroscience research, facilitated brain activity that supported a feeling of well-being. All this happened without setting one foot on French soil!

If you are recovering from an accident or lengthy illness, you can expect tremendous benefits from anticipating and even rehearsing a longed-for trip. While you plan and consider, here's what is actually happening psychologically and physiologically.

Physical pain feels diminished, and the benefits can extend for hours, when we find ways to shift attention from pain to something we anticipate with joy or something that makes us smile or laugh.

Norman Cousins, a journalist and newspaper editor in the mid 20th century, used laughter to manage chronic pain associated with his serious illness, although it was never properly diagnosed. His unique project included books and movies that made him laugh. He would focus on them non-stop for hours, blocking pain and other reminders of his situation; and, according to him, these media, always with a positive spin, provided continuous relief for extended periods of time.

Medical studies later confirmed that humor can not only reduce pain but boost the immune system while reducing stress-related hormones. Research found an additional bonus. Laughter also triggers the release of endorphins, painkillers that the body produces naturally.

Cousins later wrote, "The capacity for hope is the most significant fact of life. It provides human beings with a sense of destination and the energy to get started." He credits laughter and hope, coupled with positive anticipation of the future, for much of his recovery.

Hope is the belief that things will get better and it aids in recovery. Anticipating a positive experience enhances your mood and reduces body tension in ways similar to laughter. When you focus on the details of a future wished-for trip, good feelings grow. This stimulates neurotransmitters that boost positive mood.

You have the power to generate positive emotions that have a healing effect. You have the ability to become a more emotionally resilient person. And you can learn to withstand and rebound from psychological stress, and in some cases even physical disease. But it's critical to focus only on the pleasure, meaning and other good feelings generated.

Go ahead and anticipate your wished-for journey. Ironically, one of the advantages of a virtual trip is that it's free of the hassles often associated with real-life experience. No delayed flights, lost luggage, bad weather, or annoying companions!

Collect the travel materials that help make your future experiences real and tangible. Enjoy your anticipation!

Begin now to prepare for something pleasurable:

- Keep a journal or a bulletin board with thumb tacks.
- Try a virtual collection site like Pinterest.
- Post photos, notes, doodles, sketches, thoughts, and feelings evoked by the activity.

Reserve it for a rainy day when you need the tangible physical and psychological reminders that boost your mood and give you hope in a delightful future.

Find the good: manage disappointments and unrealistic expectations

Transform disappointment by giving your experience a new frame. Rather than focusing on what you'd wished or expected, reshape the reality of now. You might even find something to appreciate or at least balance your discontent. When travel gives you lemons, create a delicious concoction worth remembering.

My experience of Buenos Aires was at odds with the enchanted, romantic place I'd envisioned. Not long ago a thriving, thoroughly modern city, it seemed down on it's luck to me with all the concomitant problems you might anticipate; such as sidewalks with potholes, and rampant petty crime. It is sad that such a fine place, which I believe it once was, has succumbed to a difficult economy, instability and high inflation. Hopefully, better days are not far off.

Accept what is, I said to myself. Buenos Aires was deemed unsafe to explore alone by foot, and off the beaten path. "Go to the tourist areas, they are reasonably secure," echoed the concierge. But then how will I get a taste of the local culture, I wondered?

I pushed the boundaries a bit, going beyond the limitations set by conscientious guides. Since I wasn't wearing jewelry or an expensive watch, I took some geographic risks, but I was also lucky. Still, it cramped my curious style which caused some frustration. Accept this and find what's good here, I reminded myself.

The lesson here is to become aware of your preconceived notions about places so reality doesn't disappoint. I wanted Buenos Aires, Argentina to charm and intrigue but this was my wish and not the current reality. Try to understand how the place you're visiting got to be this way; feel compassion toward the place and its people.

Life and locations don't mirror Disneyland. Most places don't exist to please its visitors. As a tourist, it's my responsibility to see what *is* and to find a way to appreciate what *is*. How can you enjoy and even praise a particular destination when it doesn't meet your expectation? Start by getting yourself to see what's right not just what's wrong.

Let's go back to Buenos Aires. My ship was docked alongside a working port which gave me an opportunity to glimpse life as it really was: long shore workers unloading metal boxcars with giant cranes and hoisting the load on to long-bed trucks. This is a freighters' waterfront—no luxury cruise-liner pier at this port.

How odd it seemed. We luxuriated in the ship's breakfast service while looking out on the laborers of Buenos Aires. Ironically, some tourists lamented that they couldn't get a glimmer of the local culture because it wasn't safe to walk the streets. Yet here was a slice of it was right in front of them.

Right here in plain view, daily life showed itself—workers loading cargo. This is a sliver of life, offering a glimpse into the local dockworkers existence. Tourists can sometimes be oblivious to what is right before their eyes: not looking, not seeing, or choosing not to see.

Photo 21: Loading and unloading; dock in Buenos Aires, Argentina

It's easy to focus on glamorous Buenos Aires as it once was and miss the culture of daily life that defines a place. What is culture anyway? What makes a group of people a nation? Certainly it's a common language and nationalistic pride. It might also be the shared religion, history or community of like minded neighbors. Natural resources contribute also, in this case, a large and hospitable port.

The tango, an export from Argentina that enriched the world, originated with poor male immigrants from places like Italy, Portugal, and Spain who came to make a better life in the 19th century and used the tango to express and manage their loneliness. Their experiences colored the history and enriches life in Buenos Aires to this day. This dance, with its humble beginnings, is like a staple in the Argentinian economy. Wherever you go, couples in colorful costumes dance to entertain visitors and make some money.

Photo 23: Tango performance in Buenos Aires, Argentina

Find a way to make the most of what's offered, wherever you go, and enjoy that! Find a way to see what's right and try to de-focus on what's disappointing. You'll come away pleased and likely more satisfied. At least, that was my experience.

Making Choices

Introduction

Everyday we face endless choices in decision making. Even going down the cereal isle at the grocery becomes a cacophony of alternatives. And yet we do manage to sort and move on. Likewise, we can sift through many competing options to make decisions while traveling that best fit our goals and reduce stress.

Should I travel alone or with someone else? How do I get what I need when I'm traveling with others? How can I compromise between what I want and what I can afford? How can I reconcile competing goals? How do I find the right pace?

In the next seven mini-chapters, decision making focuses on options while traveling that are not about this or that object or destination. We'll explore different and sometimes conflicting *ways* of exploring the world.

Choose between competing goals

While walking the pristine beaches of Punta del Este, Uruguay, a majestic view of the Atlantic Ocean unfolded. Black rocks interrupted stretches of white sand. Good sized waves provided opportunities for decent surfing. High rise modern buildings along the shore contrasted with the 18th century Spanish architecture of nearby red-roofed stucco churches. A lighthouse, marking the farthest reach of La Punta, jutted out into the easternmost corner of the country.

Low and heavy rain clouds promised rain but never delivered. Instead, the weather granted me an angle of the sun that made photo taking ideal. I was glad to be alone to survey the details with my full attention—to capture the architecture, to note the way the sky and ocean met in a palate of muted blue and green shades. I watched the unfamiliar seabirds, their feathers ruffled by the steady head-on wind.

To get this moment right meant no distractions for me. Fortunately, my husband chose to follow a different sightseeing path. I'd gone off by myself to follow my own interests with my journal and pencil in hand. I wished to capture what I likely couldn't re-create at a later time. Even years later, revisiting this scene in my mind's eye helps me see once again what I found compelling.

When traveling with a group or even a friend, it's easy to miss much of the splendor. Why? Social relationships require attention. Conversation is a normal part of sightseeing, and yet it might well detract from immersion in a scene, a setting, and sensations that require focus.

You shouldn't have to choose between fully attending to your own experience and interacting with your travel companions. Both can happen, but often not at the same time. To be maximally effective requires some clarity about your goal and then sharing it with those around you.

Maybe it seems obvious, but you actually need to communicate your need for some private moments to absorb a place in your own way. Otherwise your travel buddies might inadvertently fill your available time and space. Their own needs or conversation might well lead you in some unwanted direction. Think back to some of my personal examples in previous chapters. On a number of occasions, I went off by myself leaving my husband to plan his own time. Once it was early in the morning when the rest of my travel group was still asleep.

Choosing between companions and a physical setting isn't a matter of right or wrong. It depends on your emotional or intellectual need at any moment. Taking the time to assess what's most important to you on the spot gives you the right direction. In spite of what current technology gurus leads us to believe, current scientific thinking doesn't support the claim that multi-tasking is effective. Diving deep into any one event, process, or experience has its own rewards and benefits.

The *Inward Traveler* searches for personal meaning that goes beyond a superficial nod to places. The goal isn't limited to checking the boxes: been there, done that. Mindful journeys seek to fully capture each moment to deepen experience. If you've chosen to be with others, don't become distracted by their goals. If you've chosen to take this time alone, immerse yourself in it. Find *flow*, that state of total absorption.

What's evoked by seeing a scene? Sit with your observations and focus in on details that hold some significance. Like a visual artist, frame a vision, imagine setting up an easel. Take out your imagined folding chair and position it to consider how you'd like to begin to express your creative self. This precise instant will never come again. Make it yours to remember.

Or pull out your journal. Make some notes that you may want to return to later to inspire a poem, lyrics for a song, a painting that you can picture in your mind's eye, or a sketch for a travel story. Close your eyes and listen. Feel the air temperature, the wind direction and velocity, and maybe taste salt water spray. Imagine times in the distant past when someone else sat in this precise spot. Create a story about them in your head. Play with the image. Feed your muse.

For me, being deeply absorbed in Punta de Este and the emotions evoked by that setting meant experiencing it entirely on my own. What choice might you have made? How would you have communicated that decision to a travel companion?

Set aside cravings: alternative scenarios to make travel work

Media messages bombard us daily with tales of exotic vacations and deluxe accommodations to whet our travel appetites. And it works. We create scenarios that feed our wanderlust, spinning delicious day dreams about trips we probably can't afford and likely can't execute. Perhaps you bookmark articles and photos for a future trip file, or accumulate some online images for a Pinterest page. Maybe you simply fantasize about the journeys you might someday like to take. Where does fantasy end and reality begin?

Our minds can easily conjure up a relaxing image of a warm, sunny beach or snowy mountain retreat. Such images actually slow down our breathing and help our bodies unwind. That's a healthful exercise all by itself. But bringing these images to fruition is another story. While your longing feels tangible, plans often remain elusive because the facts of your life intervene. Based on financial or time constraints, or a vague discomfort about being away from home, for example, the outcome may be doomed. But it doesn't have to be that way.

It's easy to see alternatives as black and white, in or out, all or nothing. The mind is adept at creating choices that seem crystal clear at the extremes but gray and amorphous in between. Yet the space in between actually provides rich options.

If I want a week on a tropical island, it may not happen, now or ever, for all kinds of reasons. But what about a staycation or just one private day off? This option means generally staying at home but should include special elements you crave. Let this serve as your starting point. The next step might be to find a day spa where pampering, soaking in a hot tub, swimming in a heated pool, or getting a massage are paired with soothing background music.

Does that satisfy some of the same needs? What about a big-city day trip that includes a museum visit, fine dinner, maybe a concert, but no overnight hotel cost? Will an overnight camping trip along with a trail ride by horseback partially satisfy your craving for a longer ranch stay? What other images enhance your picture, and how can you expand these for long weekends, multi-day stays?

Five and six star hotels are renowned for services as are the best of the cruise ship lines. But that comes at a cost. Know ahead that deluxe accommodations weigh heavy on a budget; or accept in advance that lower cost may possibly mean a lower quality of service—or not. But making a budget-conscious choice may have benefits. Remember, you may have to postpone travel or shelve it permanently unless you can reach a compromise that suits your budget or timeline.

Find a way to let it be OK without resentment, envy, or dis-appointment. Keeping priorities straight is one way to do that. Be clear about your goal. Why do you want to travel? What's most important to you as you consider a trip? Look inward for hidden motives that might undermine a reasonable compromise. For example, will you be traveling with others who are not financially limited? Is there anyone you feel you must impress or not disappoint? Are you worried that your enjoyment will be impaired if spending needs to be limited?

Try an experiment. Choose a hotel beneath your comfort level. Perhaps the toilet is down the hall or the management doesn't speak

English. A little risk-taking can be exciting and mastery of such a situation feels delightful.

Suppose you've always wanted to take a cruise but can't afford the financial cost, or the two weeks off from work. A repositioning cruise might be the answer and still check off the limited time and money boxes. A shorter five-day cruise up the West coast of the U.S. might board in San Diego and disembark in Vancouver, British Columbia, for example.

On a first-class cruise ship line such a trip would cost considerably less than a lengthier cruise that stops at several ports along the way. The rule of thumb is that pampering carries a high cost while basic services cost less—but on a cruise ship even basic services won't be inferior.

Here's another cruise example: A mid-range cruise ship has all kinds of accommodations. The cost is based entirely on the stateroom. All other services are virtually the same including food, entertainment, and access to recreation, library or educational on-board lectures. The penthouse traveler may be sitting next to a windowless-room vacationer but neither will know unless they share this while sitting at the same diner table. The latter may be paying as little as 25% of the cost of the most expensive digs. Yet the experience is remarkably similar.

Can you visit Las Vegas without gambling? If so, this might be another budget focused option. Much of your entertainment there is subsidized by hotels and restaurants that depend on those who can't resist a slot machine or roulette table. You may also need to bypass the stores filled with expensive clothing and art. Sure you can browse, but don't buy if you're clear about your goal.

There are other ways to make a five-star vacation happen on a modest budget. Start by setting aside unrealistic cravings and expanding "all or nothing" thinking into realistic questions like "how can I make this happen?" Now you've taken the creative first step.

Fine-tune your needs: quicken or slow the pace?

Pick a wished-for place to go. No doubt you've given it some thought. Maybe you've even planned an itinerary and daydreamed about the tiniest details, like the five-star eateries you've read about, or the sport-specific paraphernalia you'll need, including ways to pack them. So much for the logistics.

You may also have a vague idea about how you'd like to *feel* once there. Yet, how to satisfy your internal longings may not seem like a necessity that merits much attention. After all, if things go as planned, you expect to be pleased, ensuring a good time. But don't forget to factor in the possible ways to satisfy your emotional needs, which may be less obvious.

Let's say, for example, that your destination is Hawaii. It's my favorite. The 50th U.S. state is a travel destination but more importantly a metaphor for escape to paradise and peacefulness. Yet, more than an amorphous pleasure zone, the islands have distinct characteristics and cater to tourists with very diverse needs and interests.

The chain of islands that comprise Hawaii differ greatly from one another in climate, terrain and potential experience. The key to fully satisfying your current wanderlust is knowing which island and what activities to choose.

Want to de-stress or calm a busy life? Pick a more rural setting as opposed to a busy city. Kauai, for example, is the oldest in the ancient volcanic chain that comprise the 5 biggest Hawaiian Islands. It's called the Garden Island since it's had the longest run in growing vegetation and comes closest to resembling the wild, densely green and tropical setting you'd associate with stories like *Swiss Family Robinson* and *Robinson Crusoe*. These adventures tell stories of survival about shipwrecked individuals and families in the lush, but challenging, wilderness. It's also where the film *Jurassic Park* was filmed.

Kauai is the least populated of the tourist destinations and offers the greatest number of hidden beaches and mountain hikes through pristine, overgrown vegetation. It might be perfect if you're seeking solitude in breathtaking beauty and uncrowded places. It's also a writer's or artist's dream-setting for generating and massaging creative material.

On the other hand, if you want to excite or stimulate a sluggish feeling, an urban place like Honolulu on the island of Oahu might be the perfect choice. While Oahu is only the third largest island in size, it is home to two-thirds of the state's population including Hawaii's capital city, Honolulu. Much of Oahu, however, is rural and as relaxed as a Hawaiian slack-key guitar tune!

Honolulu is a major city with everything you might expect in New York, London or Chicago. In this kind of setting the rich night life parallels the daytime's array of energizing offerings but without any formality. It's surrounded by continuously warm ocean waters, humid breezes, and unending palm trees of every size and description. Brilliantly colored exotic birds feel perfectly at home in spite of the noisy tumult.

Beyond the setting, whether rural or metropolitan, consider the *pace* of your vacation. Being in an energizing setting for days at a time can sharpen your thinking and quicken your emotions—which may be exactly what you need. Or not.

Consider the opposite. A slow pace in an environment with fewer cues can inspire more creative thinking because the background is softer, less demanding on your senses. That allows your imagination to take center stage, uninterrupted. Start by thinking about your stress level and whether your mood has been more sluggish or over-stimulated. Stress is useful up to a certain point beyond which it interferes with health and well-being. Take a daily gut reading by noticing your internal state and energy level, then tailor your pace up or down.

Even within a given environment there are ways to fine-tune the tempo to match your needs. Suppose you are in midtown New York City, but craving a way to wind down the over-stimulation? A short bus ride can land you in Central Park with miles of paths and more trees and green space than you can navigate by foot in a week of walking. This gives you the setting and tone in which to create a peaceful moment right in the middle of one of the busiest places on earth.

Feed your passion or curiosity: travel with a specific theme

Are you a history buff? Are you an engineer at heart who loves to understand how things work? Does your adventuresome spirit lead you to remote sites where most of the visitors are bears? This chapter explores an approach that requires immersion. In-depth, intensive activities satisfy a different kind of wanderlust. Think vertical rather than horizontal, deep not broad. There are countless thematic journeys.

The most obvious starting point is a place that once piqued your curiosity when you heard or read about it. Identify a narrow but in-depth focus rather than trying to spread yourself thin by seeing more in limited time.

What about travel combined with charity, science/archeology digs, religious quests, or education? Once again, start with your passion or curiosity.

Did you once want to be an anthropologist looking for clues to early human markers that still needs unearthing? Maybe it was an impractical goal earlier in your life, but now you can join a "dig" as a volunteer, travel to dusty, rural sites and search for fragments that help solve puzzles about long-gone inhabitants. If this sounds like you, the starting point is an online search for university sponsored projects that include volunteers.

Similarly, if your penchant is building houses for needy people that taps your inner architect or carpenter, consider former President

Jimmy Carter's[5] non-profit organization *Habitat for Humanity*. Volunteer labor makes up a work force that builds and rehabilitates homes in the U.S. and abroad for grateful individuals. It was popularized many years ago by President Carter and former first lady, Rosalyn, in their search for meaningful ways to do good deeds after they left the White House. Below is a link which will be your starting point: http://www.habitat.org/how/carter.aspx.

Consider educational opportunities at universities worldwide that welcome aspiring adults to brick and mortar campuses or to on-line virtual ones. Some educational travel includes onsite lectures by experts. Consider *Road Scholars*, a not-for-profit learning organization with destination themes that guide "generations of knowledge seekers on transformative learning adventures." They've been around for ages, originally known as Elderhostel (1975). Here is the link: https://www.roadscholar.org/roadscholar-experience/mission-history/.

Or, pick a place that resonates with deeply held feelings. Do you favor exotic jungles, or enormous cranes and other mega-machines? Are you yearning to farm like some of your ancestors? Or maybe work as a ranch hand for a week on the open plains of Wyoming? Perhaps a ship journey, that within a day traverses the distance between the Atlantic and Pacific Oceans, is your cup of tea? If that's not enough, how about a place where the sun appears to rise in the west and set in the east—opposite of what seems normal? You probably guessed the Panama Canal, and you'd be correct.

---

[5] *Habitat for Humanity* was co-founded by Millard and Linda Fuller

Crossing the Panama Canal appeals to a variety of tastes from the engineering geek to the history buff. Panama itself is a lovely tropical country but also an isthmus (a narrow strip of land bound by seas on both sides). It's attraction throughout the ages is its unique geography bound on one side by the Atlantic Ocean and the Pacific Ocean hugging the other shore.

Throughout the ages, this isthmus seemed perfectly situated for a shipping passage. Making that happen was the obsession of more that a few engineers and countries for centuries. Its completion would avoid a detour around South America, saving many thousands of miles for European vessels headed for the U.S.A. west coast or Asia.

The history of the Panama Canal spans hundreds of years, and was as much lore as an actual project for much of that time. In the 1500's Spanish king Francis sent an expedition party to map and plan a canal. But it took more than 300 years for it to actually be completed with many stops and starts in between. The sacrifices of life to disease and the challenges of cutting through tropical foliage atop volcanic rock make history read like fiction. This is a journey that can appeal to a couple with very dissimilar interests, and yet satisfy both.

What makes a trip worth taking, and how do you pick from all the possibilities? The most obvious starting point is a place that once piqued your curiosity when you heard or read about it.

A trip through the Panama Canal gives you a first hand look at a place that changed the outcome of history. Imagine if cargo and passenger ships still had to circumnavigate South America around Cape Horn to

Photo 24: Locks closing at the Panama Canal

get from the east coast of the U.S.A., Europe or Africa to the West coast of the Northern Hemisphere? I made the elongated trip via the route tracing South America's perimeter. Though less dangerous than a century before, it was still fraught with weather and climate dangers—but, thankfully, no pirates! Yes, it's also a worthy trip but not for everyone!

Pick your theme and get going. Start local, in your neighborhood, or go for a big exploration. The choice is yours, the rewards are intrinsic.

Solo travel: new behavior or preferred approach

Just because you have a partner doesn't mean your trip will be improved by taking him or her along. The advantages of going with a travel companion are obvious: you're seldom alone and you don't need to make all of the decisions by yourself. These may also become some of the downsides. Traveling alone allows you to have access to many more thoughts and sensations that may be blocked when distracted by a second person or group.

Seeing a place, hearing its sounds, noticing its smells, its textures, or the feelings evoked requires sensitivity to your own internal processes. You form impressions and then let them percolate as you daydream. Your ongoing internal dialogue, known as your stream of consciousness, takes your observations and impressions and forms stories. Alone, there's no one else to affect the story development you create.

Understanding the local culture, or the way people relate to each other requires the kind of attention that's difficult to arrange in a duo or crowd. People watching is primarily a solo sport. At least that is my experience.

Many years ago I spent two months alone teaching at a university in Switzerland. The following year I went again to the same town, Lugano, a dreamy, sun kissed, mountainside city, in the southern Italian sector of Switzerland. But this time my husband came along. I was amazed at the difference between the two experiences.

On my solo excursion, I was much more sensitive to everything I saw and interpreted it through my own lens in a kind of ongoing reverie or dream-like state. I didn't interact with others too much while traveling, but enjoyed being an observer. If I felt social, I was comfortable talking to others, as well as language gaps permitted. But mostly I watched, which I enjoyed immensely. Of course this is most pleasurable if you're an introverted type, which I am. (More about introversion/extraversion in the next section.)

The second journey, a shared experience, colored all that I encountered entirely differently, though not better or worse. I sometimes wished I were alone to fully immerse my attention as I had done the year before. Other times I was grateful for the company. It's a mixed bag.

If you are by yourself, when and if loneliness creeps in, you'll notice heightened motivation to talk to strangers you would ordinarily not do, perhaps leading to new behavior. Even if it's painfully uncomfortable to reach out and start a conversation, your need for contact at that moment will likely override any discomfort. And remember, contact is generally going to be limited in an accidental meeting, like two ships going in different directions. Knowing that you'll never encounter this person again may give you the courage to interact. Nothing to lose!

Or arrange a trip so that days are alone but dinner is with others. Cruises, spas, language schools, dude ranches, tennis camp, music camp, and spiritual retreats are some venues that allow for solo travel but shared moments when you're in the mood.

Experiment with solo travel by starting small. Plan a day trip when your usual companions aren't available. Try a museum, art exhibit opening in a gallery, daytime movie, solo lunch, or dinner. Notice your feelings and observations. Going solo in a paired up culture may lead to some self-critical judgments that feel painful. Let them surface and then decide if any of these is valid before taking them in. You may find that you actually like going alone!

Shared travel: deepen good relationships or renew stale ones

Whether a solo act or partnered, we all get into relationship ruts occasionally. It's easy to take your best friend or life partner for granted and become careless in communicating with him or her.

Much of daily life is routine and highly scheduled. Doing the same things in a predictable way can trigger stale responses and knee-jerk reactions to partners with unhappy outcomes. For example, if you tend to rush around while getting ready in the morning, or at dinner time, and this makes you irritable, the person nearest to you will likely feel your negative energy and react defensively.

Repeated on a daily basis, the same old prompts lead to the same old responses. But time away from day-in and day-out patterns affects both what we do and how others react to it. Enter travel as a way to refresh relationships by removing many of the cues that trigger bad behavior.

Whatever your life situation, whether you are a student, a working person, or in the post-work phase of your life, daily life becomes predictable. There's no way around it. It takes way too much psychological energy to act as if every event or interaction is novel. We use short cuts in sizing up a situation. If it looks familiar, we tend to respond as if it is. Sometimes you may be rushed but not irritable, and yet your partner may still act defensively, misreading the familiar behavior.

At home it's easy to snap at your live-in companion about undone daily maintenance chores. Disappointed expectations, like why the trash wasn't taken out, promise to irritate. Incomplete or misinterpreted communication while on the run can result in misunderstandings and hurt feelings. Many of these interactions are patterns that get reinforced on a daily basis unless something changes them, like taking a trip.

Travel introduces just enough novelty to interfere with old annoying patterns. Even when the stress of traveling is present, the irritants are usually sufficiently different so that common conflicts don't arise in the same ways. For example, finding a metro stop in an unfamiliar city becomes a shared concern but doesn't trigger irritation at a partner since the both of you may be clueless. The daily annoyances from back home tend to get suspended, allowing space for new ways of communicating to emerge.

Develop, increase, or rekindle intimacy more easily, as a possible by-product of shared travel. My husband likes to remind me that it's difficult to get close to a porcupine or barking dog. What I think he means is that when I'm criticizing or blaming him for something he's done wrong, or not done at all, he tries to stay clear of me. That scenario doesn't foster closeness. When we travel, and the familiar irritants are left at home, we interact more positively. Look for opportunities to get closer while traveling. Consider some of the following suggestions:

- In advance, talk about your own, as well as shared, goals and preferences.

- Begin a trip with the mindset that you'll monitor your own behavior more closely. Note any irritants, but attempt to take a few breaths to keep from responding automatically.

- Start your day by remembering the good qualities of your traveling companion. Recall the reasons you wanted to travel with him/her in the first place.

- Spend at least one-half hour each day in eye-to-eye and face-to-face interaction without attending to an electronic/interactive device. This may actually feel too intense so back off to fewer minutes as necessary to get started.

- Engage in trouble-free conversation—no blaming or criticizing about jobs undone or done incorrectly. Focus on what's good, positive, and working well.

Illustration 3: Face to face communication with travel partner

Travel following loss: find wellsprings of comfort and peace

Life is dynamic and ever changing which incudes our most meaningful relationships. Sadly, loss is inevitable as time goes by. There's no right way to grieve the loss of a love. But when the pain subsides enough to create some space, options for renewal present themselves.

Travel is one way to handle and explore the potential emptiness. It doesn't require lots of money, time, or a spirit of adventure. The goal is simply to change the pattern of daily living to encourage new, and maybe more sustainable habits going forward, without your special person. But the first step is compassion for your hurting soul.

Intellectually, this makes sense, but nothing prepares us emotionally for the inevitable sadness and grief, natural and necessary in the recovery process. The passage of time helps dull the pain. But soothing an aching heart, while holding warm and deep memories, might include a time-out for rejuvenation and recuperation. With reminders lurking everywhere you turn, how can you possibly maintain your equilibrium when your love is gone? Once again, travel may help.

The physical environment and your thoughts offer constant reminders of the one who is no longer there. Whether it's your life partner, your parent, or furry best friend, you will continue to hold them dear, with or without the familiar cues being nearby. Getting away for a while doesn't mean forgetting.

Travel that provides comfort and soothing isn't primarily about the destination, but the healing and nurturing atmosphere it provides. The place you pick needs to feel safe and at the same time satisfy your spiritual or emotional needs. While it will whisk you away from the reminders it also gives you a respite from despair.

If you've always traveled with someone dear who's now departed from your life, it might be hard for you to consider traveling again without them. Listen to your inner voice. Would there be comfort in finding a place that's new to you, without the familiar markers of your time together? What would your partner say about you traveling now? If you aren't ready for anything extensive, a local journey, maybe to the science museum or zoo you've always intended to visit, could be just right.

Remember, your goal is a health seeking time-out from suffering so that you can return somewhat restored and better able to adapt to your changed life. Knowing yourself, what do you think would work for you?

What about a religious retreat in a quiet monastery? For this option you don't necessarily need to be a religious person. You might consider a Catholic retreat where your basic needs are met in a simple environment, with the added benefit of silence or space for prayer or meditation. Maybe a Buddhist hideaway is your answer, offering similar comforts.

Another option is a peaceful haven like Mt. Madonna, in northern California, (https://www.mountmadonna.org). This is "a place where you can step back, slow down, and reconnect to your center, and to nature." A yoga oriented center, it is surrounded by redwood trees in the Santa Cruz mountains. Food is simple, vegetarian, and beautifully presented in an atmosphere where you can choose silence or quiet conversation, depending on your needs. Similar places exist throughout the U.S.A. and abroad. Some allow stays as brief as one day.

Consider a pamper and health focused spa like Rancho La Puerta in Tecate, Mexico (http://www.rancholapuerta.com). One of my favorites, it offers a tranquil setting nestled close to Mt. Kuchumaa in Baja, California. As a wellness center, it provides fitness options through organized classes, and organic meals. But it also fosters spiritual self care through silence when needed, and group hikes to majestic mountain peaks. Yoga is also available as a mind/body tonic. All of this in a spa atmosphere with saunas, hot tubs, massage and aromatherapy.

 Perhaps a service-focused mission is the right choice for you. As mentioned in a previous chapter, "Habitat for Humanity," (http://www.habitat.org) was fostered by President Jimmy Carter and his wife Rosalyn. It offers volunteer opportunities to help build homes for families demonstrating a need for affordable housing (who also participate in "400 hours of sweat equity"). Giving service in this way, and partnering with others to improve their circumstances, feels good. It also shifts the focus away from your own pain and suffering, while providing a healthy time-out.

What about participating in a targeted outcome trip such as an archaeological dig, mentioned earlier? Opportunities are available around the globe and possibly close to home. According to the Archaeological Institute of America, "Each year thousands of students and volunteers go into the field to experience an excavation firsthand,

and the Archaeological Fieldwork Opportunities Bulletin (AFOB) helps them find a project." This is another service-giving journey to do something worthwhile and personally meaningful. Like all the other healing travels, giving yourself in this way shifts the focus of your attention away from sadness, in a wholesome environment. See (https://www.archaeological.org/fieldwork).

Of course, none of these options substitutes for normal grieving. But all of them give you needed respite with healthy activities in supportive surroundings. Time and a nurturing home-based community will likely take care of the rest.

Mind and Emotions at Work

Introduction

The final section of the *Inward Traveler* explores additional ways of knowing and exploring your inner world by trying out new or evolving aspects of yourself. You can always find ways to fine-tune behaviors, or expand your comfort level with new foods and different ways, to present yourself anytime and anyplace. But it's sure easier to take these kind of risks away from home, away from routine, away from the familiar. Let's explore the internal change process traveling can evoke.

If you're an Introvert, you might want to try extroverting. If you are a fussy eater, take baby steps to expand your food repertoire. If you're the serious type, learn how to play more. If you're able to focus intently on an experience, can you also comfortably let go and give in to distraction? Exercising these opposites gives flexibility to your brain's functioning. Just like the muscles in your body, a malleable brain that continues to learn will enhance your life and strengthen your mind.

Introvert or Extravert: navigate the journey your own way

Finding a balance between people and places is one key to satisfaction while on the road. This is especially true if your travel companions have a personality style that differs from your own. If traveling with friends or family appeals to you—and the more the merrier, you're probably an Extravert. But some folks cringe at the idea of being trapped on a bus with others for hours or days at a time without escape to alone time and space.

There is no particular advantage in being an Introvert or an Extravert, and neither is psychologically healthier or happier. But Introverts, sometimes literally, aren't happy campers when forced to stay in social situations longer than they prefer. Extraverts, on the other hand, don't intuitively understand this need for solitude. So, mismatches in style can create havoc in any shared experience, especially if it's extended beyond a few hours!

When I'm alone, I'm invigorated and do my most creative thinking. A solo hike in the natural beauty of nearby hills leaves me feeling inspired and restored. It's especially joyful when I'm tired or weary from too many commitments. For me, the solo experience itself creates a high. It is unspoiled by others' chatter and the reminders of the to-do lists, life's problems or the need to take in and attend to the words of my companions. Another way to say this is that I am in a state of flow[6]. In the silence I have the freedom to access my inner muse and fully delight in the physical world.

---

[6] See definition, page 27

As I walk alone one morning on a popular trail that borders a reservoir, chatting families pass by. Mothers talk on cell phones deep into their conversations while pushing running-strollers. They're probably relieved to have a few minutes to speak undisturbed without worrying about a toddler getting into any trouble. Perhaps this is the only exercise they get which makes multi-tasking a reasonable goal. But much goes unnoticed, like the natural world of spotted ground squirrels digging nearby, and the occasional crane posing on one leg for anyone who might be looking.

Further along on this hike, I see pairs and trios of middle aged folks walking, occasionally slowing down to acknowledge the sights. For these friends, the walk is a bonus but often not the main event—which may be more to socialize and catch up on time gone by. They walk the walk and experience satisfaction and pleasure; but unlike me, much of their invigoration comes from contact with others. Both Introverts and Extraverts enjoy the company of people, but for different reasons.

For Extraverts, sharing time with people is a high priority that makes all other experiences richer and more satisfying. Extraverts almost never tire of being with others and in fact get renewed and revitalized in this way. I haven't done a survey, but I would bet that anyone walking alone looking deep in thought is not an Extravert.

Introverts enjoy others, but in small doses, and preferably when they've had their fill of solitude or quiet times with close/intimate companions. Introverts have the necessary skills to be sociable and appreciate people, especially when they know they can retreat to their private space when they've had enough contact.

Introverts will gladly share your time if they can go off by themselves to explore, and/or if it is a time-limited excursion and they know they will have a chance to be refreshed by their own company after a while. Introverts become uncomfortable when dragged along to a follow-up social event. Of course, for Extraverts, a quiet evening can seem like torture unless it follows a day of intense partying.

Knowing who you are and what you need in terms of space and quiet is a necessity and a good starting point. Communicating about your I or E style with fellow travelers, even if the trip is short, reduces the chances for misunderstanding or hurt feelings that can throw a trip out of alignment.

If you are still not sure whether you are an Introvert or Extravert, here's a link (http://fortune.com/2015/06/03/cain-introvert-quiz/) to a brief quiz from *Fortune Magazine*, based on the work of Susan Cain author of the book, *Quiet: The Power of Introverts in a World that Can't Stop Talking*. This is a good way to get a quick and approximate assessment of your own personality style.

Overcome self-perceived limitations

When I was a young teen, I wished that I could disappear from my current life and emerge somewhere where people didn't know me. My vague angst wasn't tied to anything in particular. It's not that I wanted to be someone I idolized, or to escape from a dangerous situation.

My longing was simply an escape fantasy. In this version of my life, all the burdens of an unfamiliar body, teen-girl dramas and personal limitations, like shyness, would dissolve. It's not uncommon for adolescents to feel dissatisfied with themselves and their surroundings. You may have some similar memories from your own life.

In my wished-for scenario I would re-emerge as outgoing and comfortable with new people in new situations. Alas, it didn't happen back then, though I did try role playing new characters and even tried to shed the New York accent I'd inherited. It was to no avail. In real life, people and circumstances surrounding me reinforced the old accent, and the painful status quo of my current reality.

But I learned through travel that I really could try out new behaviors uncharacteristic of me, and wouldn't be judged by those I met. No one I ever encountered along the way knew about my anxieties or self-perceived social limitations. I could be anyone I pleased, which gave me permission to try on new ways of being, from accent tweaking to greater assertiveness and social comfort.

Become more outgoing while on the road if that is your goal. Everyone you encounter is a stranger, unlikely to be seen again, so there's greater safety for you to take more risks in what you say and do. Social mistakes in one-time meetings carry fewer consequences. Introverts like me can take this on, as long as we can retreat to our quiet space to regenerate energy expended while extroverting.

Maybe you can identify with the feelings of an awkward teenager or adult and would like to try out some new ways of being with people, only without embarrassment or self-judgment. Your traveling companions might be surprised, but hopefully their observations will be judgment-free.

Learn to suspend your own self-limiting perceptions. Approaching strangers is a learnable skill, and trying on wished-for social behaviors is not only possible but an effective strategy. But first you need to acknowledge your perceived deficits, accept that they are a current part of your repertoire, and understand that how you interact and respond is limited only by your self-judgments.

It's easy enough to picture yourself being uncomfortable, but can you imagine a scenario in which you are unselfconscious, open to approaching someone or to their overture when their eyes meet yours? The remedy is quite simple, but you need practice!

Here's a "new behavior" experiment to carry out in the privacy of your own home. Find ten minutes. Close your eyes and allow your breathing to slow and deepen. As you begin to relax, create an action scene in your head in which you are the main character and actor. What does it look like? Pick something within the realm of possibility, like striking up a conversation with a seat-mate on a train trip or long flight. Can you rehearse it as if you were acting in a play that you wrote? Can you describe the situation and the person you've chosen to interact with? What makes them seem welcoming to you? What's the risk? What's the benefit?

In this scenario, it helps to place yourself in a setting that is new to you so that familiar cues don't evoke the same old fearful or unwanted responses. For this context or setting, use your imagination or recall a photo from a travel brochure that you came across. Try out a few different performances. Pick the one that seems closest to your goals and isn't a huge stretch for you to accomplish. Remember that people will respond to you based on your actual behavior, not on your worries or fears.

Shaping new behavior goes well beyond meeting new people while traveling. It also includes trying out different foods, adapting to a different culture, fine-tuning your likes and dislikes whatever they may be, and even going separate ways from your travel companions if only for a couple of hours or half day.

Expand your tastes and preferences

Some years ago, I eagerly opted for a four-day layover in Hong Kong where I planned to wander the city by myself. In those days, there were no direct flights from Singapore to San Francisco, and the plane change in Hong Kong gave me a unique opportunity to visit an exotic place on my bucket list.

This brief adventure promised to be exciting. Hong Kong had been a British colony until shortly before my visit, with Chinese foundations and intriguing Asian cuisine and customs. I hoped that my English would be sufficient since it is my only proficient language. I imagined that all the markers were in place for a perfect first visit.

I hastily booked a basic hotel that met my needs for economy. And because of the cultural and ethnic diversity of the guests, mostly European and Asian, I imagined I might get to expand my understanding of diverse customs just by watching.

Most of what I expected turned out to be wishful thinking. The reality was quite different but even a better learning opportunity because of that. Almost immediately I realized that since the 99-year lease to the British had expired a few years before, Chinese was now the primary language and the country was quick to revert to its native tongue.

Not far from the waterfront that separates Hong Kong island from Kowloon, I realized that I could use the ferry to get back and forth to my hotel on the mainland. Thankfully, the distinctive skyline kept me oriented. Since the familiar English language cues were mostly absent, I found myself in an unfamiliar city, alone, with no way to communicate or decipher Chinese long before electronic maps and translators. Travel can be a wonderful teacher when you're paying attention.

Hong Kong is one of those photographic places that makes it easily recognizable. I thought, good, I'll rely on visual cues and won't need language so much. This worked for well-known destinations like Victoria Peak, high above the city and easily identifiable. It proved to be the highlight of my trip, easy to reach via the tram/funicular, revealing spectacular, panoramic views of the city and lush semi-tropical vegetation that practically scraped the sides of the aerial coach.

Photo 25: Looking down on Hong Kong harbor from Victoria Peak

So much for visual cues! These were totally absent in my search for the famous Night Market which opened at 10 PM in another part of the city. With my failure to grasp the subway system, I walked for miles following directions from my English language travel guidebook, which proved to be woefully out of date.

When I finally found my way, I was exhausted but enthralled by the traditional practices. Caged birds would tell your fortune by pecking at and picking up cards in their beaks. Old men with gray goatees played music on Chinese stringed instruments in scales and chords that seemed strange and enchanting. What a treat! I still carry those images in my head when I think of Hong Kong. As I write these lines, pleasant memories bubble up and wash over me.

Photo 26: Night Market crowded between buildings in Hong Kong

But it wasn't all delightful. I'm not much of a shopper, but I wandered over to Nathan Avenue, the renowned shopping street where you can buy anything. It's famous for custom apparel like men's and women's suits, measured on your body and ready for pickup in only two days.

Shoved along by huge crowds of people, as if I'd landed on a human conveyer belt, the visceral memories are not pleasant. Although I'm from New York City, I wasn't prepared for the density of people on this street and was quick to extract myself. Not my preferred way to spend time. Good to know.

As you might expect, the food was delightful, representing a blending of Southeast Asian cultures. But since I had to order by pointing to pictures that showed only Chinese characters that I can't read, I didn't know then, nor can I tell you now exactly what I ate.

According to scientific evidence, our comfort with new foods tends to decrease as we age, and our repertoire usually becomes more narrow and limited to what's familiar. This was true for me. Experimenting with food proved more anxiety producing than I expected. Also good to know.

I learned as much about my likes and dislikes in this travel experience as I did about Hong Kong. It helped inform my current tastes and future choices, which is, after all, one benefit of traveling.

What's the takeaway message here?

- Understand your baseline. Are you naturally adventuresome or do you like to stick with the familiar? That is your starting point. Honor your own perceptions. For fussy eaters, or to honor timid or limited palates, start with small changes. That might mean experimenting with just one morsel of food, or wandering only in the neighborhood of your home-away-from-home, or sticking to hotel restaurants. That still might be a stretch and make sure to appreciate your effort.

- Try on new things for size, but you don't need to own them—and I don't mean just clothing. Be open to learning. But you don't necessarily have to like what you learn and can back away from it, or reject it outright, if a taste, literally or metaphorically, seems repugnant. If you aren't comfortable learning some words in another language, don't. Even if you learn a few words, like a greeting, you don't have to speak it out loud or to anyone else—unless and until you're ready.

- If you do choose to learn a few words, "thank you" is a good start.

How time perspective affects travel: do you live in the past, present or future?

As an enjoyable vacation winds down, some of us become impatient to get home and move on to the next thing. Maybe that's you. But you might also be someone who tries to preserve, or even expand, every remaining moment. In either case, you'll attempt to lock these precious flashes into your memory bank with mental snapshots. But the present quickly fades into the past.

How we experience time is relevant to travel because it's a limited or even scarce commodity. Understanding your time perspective can enhance your experience by adding another dimension.

Retired Stanford University professor Phil Zimbardo, author of *The Time Paradox*, notes that we are all oriented to time in one of following characteristic ways—past, present, or future. According to his profile, I am future oriented. What might your style be? Let's see.

Those of us in the *future* category are goal driven, focused on the future consequences of our actions, and forward looking in general. As you might guess, *present-hedonic* folks are the pleasure seekers who enjoy things in real time, with less concern about tomorrow. Folks who live in the *present* tend to be open to experience that they didn't necessarily plan and they don't need to check it off their bucket list. If this style fits, you're probably most content with the moment-to-moment flow of your travel.

Past-oriented people make up the remaining category. This might be you if you compare current experiences with memories of past events or situations. Past-oriented folks determine the value of travel, according to Dr. Zimbardo, by assigning a pleasure quotient to the comparison—better or worse and by how much? This style is more analytic, rational, and based less on emotional factors than is true for present focused folks. Does this sound like you?

Our characteristic types are neither good nor bad, just different from one another. Future and past oriented travelers provide a logical, systematic understanding of where travel fits into human experience. These styles have great evolutionary value. Our distant ancestors, who chronicled the past and predicted the future, tended to be the shaman and story tellers of the tribe. Reviewing the past and predicting the future was critical to human survival.

Present oriented people tend to have more fun in the moment; and every society needs this type of person to keep things from getting too serious. Savoring the present is an acquired skill and is worth the effort to cultivate! Also, by expanding the present-pleasant and then reviewing a trip in the past-positive you can have both good feelings and pleasurable memories. Since, as Dr. Zimbardo's research indicates, we have characteristic ways of perceiving time, maintaining a present-focus may require some work—if this isn't naturally how you see the world.

Zimbardo points to another dimension of time—one that is age related. In general, children are present oriented while adults favor the future. Seniors tend to preserve the past. As a future focused senior I'm aware of the need to put my foot on the brake and try to prolong the present—particularly the pleasing moments while vacationing.

Regardless of the type that best explains you, here are some strategies to expand your time orientation:

- If you're naturally drawn to the *past* or *future*, notice these tendencies and gently nudge yourself toward the present moment. When you catch yourself reminiscing about the last time you were in Paris, as you sit at an outdoor café savoring your steaming latte and munching on a croissant, remind yourself that the people you see strolling by are there right now—not last time or next time. The weather is uniquely now, not needing a contrast with a warmer or sunnier last visit. The present can be pleasant without any backward reference—or simply less.

- *Future* oriented travelers tend to spend their present moments imagining future trips, which makes sense in planning life, but can steal from the here-and-now. Recently, on a river cruise through Austria, I was struck by how much conversation I overheard about planning the next trip. Busily sharing these thoughts with fellow travelers, these vacationers sat by a large picture window as the ship taxied into a new city—totally missing the present moment, unnoticed outside of the window.

- Again, if future is your natural mode, keep that in mind as you travel. Learn to prolong the only moment that truly exists—this one that you anticipated for months or maybe years. The first step involves gently guiding your awareness back to the present. Practicing meditation even a few minutes a day will make this process easier.

Travel impacts the brain and psyche: modify your brain's structure and function

Take a trip to shake up your psyche. Go somewhere that forces you to reason and act differently in order to cope. Stretch outside of your comfort zone because that can benefit your brain as much as a vigorous workout at the gym. Plus, the concentration and focus required leads to *flow*—and a timeless place of contentment. Some changes might even become permanent—creating new thoughts, feelings and even reshaping your conscious mind.

If you are a city person, try camping in the wilderness. It needn't be as extreme as Cheryl Strayed who documented her life-changing ordeal in the book, *Wild: From Lost to Found on the Pacific Crest Trail*: "Escape the beaten path: wilderness travel," referred to earlier in this book.

If your comfort zone is rural or suburban, try a week in New York City with non-stop action 24/7. The point is to take a time out from sameness in a novel and maybe an uncomfortable setting. You can challenge old standby patterns, allowing new patterns to emerge.

There was a time, only a few decades ago, when common knowledge held that the brain was a fixed entity. When I was in graduate school, a half century ago, I learned that the brain continues to develop until around age 30 when a gradual decline begins as neuronal production stops—a slippery slope. End of story. Change in how we viewed, experienced, and interpreted the world seemed unimaginable.

Changing the brain's structure and functioning was once thought impossible, but today neuroscientists believe it is highly likely under the right circumstances. Changing our outlook and behaviors in our middle or later years, does in fact continue to alter the brain's functioning and structure. Travel provides some of the right combinations for stimulating brain change and maintaining its sharpness.

This process is called *neuroplasticity* and means what it sounds like: the brain is malleable and like plastic can be shaped and reshaped throughout the course of our lives. But, of course, this depends on the kind of stimulation the brain receives and new inputs, not easy to come by in predictable and routine lifestyles and environments. "Use it or lose it" applies to the brain just as much as to other parts of the body.

Right now there's ample scientific evidence that people who continue to use their brains, especially as they age, in *novel, complex,* and *problem solving* ways don't show the kind of cognitive decline once thought to be inevitable. There are lots of ways to keep the brain active and flexible. Similar to the physical body, exercise is good. Beyond maintaining cognitive flexibility, changing old ways of thinking and doing is both possible and healthy.

Travel is an ideal and pleasurable way to undo fixed patterns in the brain. Think about a jar of colored marbles. Jiggle the jar and the design is altered, not necessarily better or worse. What about a kaleidoscope through which you see an array of shifting designs and colors? Rotate the tube and a new pattern emerges. Likewise, modify your routines and some fixed patterns begin to recombine.

Even if you've traveled the world and run out of new places to visit, your next foray might be to someplace familiar—but this time with a fresh approach. It's a way to stimulate your brain and transform your journey.

The benefits of a distracted mind: when focus gets in the way

Children are masters of play. They focus where their attention takes them and only for brief periods. What if we took a lesson from them? Can you imagine taking a playful approach to things while traveling? Suppose you decided to take the whole experience less seriously. Maybe flitter from thing to thing without much thought or conscious planning. Wander about to see what attracts you rather than follow an itinerary.

Can you enjoy the mindset of a two-year-old who has a two-minute attention span? It would mean letting go of your observing ego, that part of your mind that monitors and critiques your behavior. You might try to suspend the rules, other than good judgment of course.

Go where your instinct and physical senses take you. Follow the smell your nose detects, notice a curious sound, or feel the texture of fuzzy leafed plant. Maybe track something that you spotted out of the corner of your eye—a color, a movement, a spoken word, or an interesting object.

You've heard that focusing is healthy—and good for your psyche. It gives your mind a rest from constant chatter. It's also good for your body because it supports slow, deep, breathing, and relaxation. Concentration allows your brain to conserve its energy for the object of your attention. Whether it's playing a game of bridge, writing in a diary, or sketching a flower, focus gives you a momentary time out from the busy world and multi-tasking.

But ironically the opposite is also true. Loosening your focus has benefits. It can help you to become a more creative problem solver.

Recent research on distractibility suggests just that. A psychology professor at the University of Toronto found that "there are things that people learn faster and remember better when they are not exercising careful control over what they're doing."

At the University of Pennsylvania, according to the *Wall Street Journal*, psychological research by Dr. Sharon Thompson-Schill showed that "when people exert less cognitive control, they become better at generating ideas." That's the benefit of letting your mind wander— it stimulates your creative juices.

How might you apply this finding to your journey? Take some time and enliven your outing with a toddler's curiosity. When you've given it a fair trial, return to this chapter to debrief. What did you learn? How did it improve or interfere with your day? Did you notice any new connections between your unfocused behavior and novel thoughts, ideas, or problem solving strategies?

Not comfortable in throwing all plans and cautions to the wind? In that case, it might feel more comfortable to set aside an hour or two to experiment with this idea. Be distracted but inform any travel partners about this exercise in advance, or include one or more as playmates. Going solo is also fine.

This is my experience: On a recent trip to Puerto Vallarta, Mexico I took an early morning walk on the beach leaving my companions to their sleep. Strolling along the water's edge and feeling the waves wash over my feet, I noticed some shells, not especially remarkable, but I picked them up anyway and continued meandering. Then I saw the remnants of a sand castle that had barely survived overnight, intact. Sitting down next to it, I first arranged my shells and then dug patterns in the sand with their scalloped edges.

Suddenly an hour had passed. I looked up from my design which had grown quite intricate. None of this was planned but all of it was original and creative, at least in my mind. I was as proud of my handiwork as any five-year-old. I also came away with some ideas about how to structure some writing that had me stuck—my mind was at work all along even though I was distracted.

Let go of logic, order, and predictability for a little while and see what you can create.

Success increases confidence: an adventure in baby steps

If your idea of a good time includes a picnic lunch and bird watching in the local park, very little tweaking is necessary to satisfy your wanderlust. But if you long to have adventure beyond the county boundaries and can't get yourself started, you might want to identify some of the blocks that keep you stuck.

If you listen wistfully when friends describe their travels but you can't commit to going far, take some time to sort out the reasons. Once identified, the blocks can be successfully challenged. Taking things slowly is the key to changing all behavior.

While this chapter is about travel, it's also metaphorical—success of any stripe increases confidence. Sure, there are theories that emphasize throwing yourself head first into experiences that are beyond your tolerances. It's like diving into cold water hoping you'll recover from the shock—and want to do it again! Not very likely.

I prefer the method that keeps adding tiny experiences, hardly noticeable, but that cumulatively result in big changes. For example, let's say that you are a finicky eater or limited in your culinary experience, an idea introduced in Chapter 47 (see table of contents). Is that what's getting in the way of leaving your comfort zone?

Not being able to count on the food being familiar and predictable can be a trip stopper. It's a limitation that makes it hard to consider places with different palates and customs—not because you're stubborn or rigid but out of real discomfort or fear of going hungry, or embarrassing yourself. What if they served you fish eyeballs or chicken feet? Not so unusual in parts of China.

To further hone in on the problem, imagine that you'd like to go to China, but you don't speak Cantonese or Mandarin and worry that you won't be able to identify what you're being served. You've heard that the Chinese eat every part of every living thing—which they do. It makes you squeamish.

Now imagine that you can find some options in China to help you feel less uneasy. That was my experience when I traveled with a group of mostly Chinese Americans and Chinese Canadians who intercepted my food as it was served to identify it before it got to me! My experience was accidental and good fortune. What might you choose to do in that situation?

Here's another option. If you live near a big city like New York, Chicago or San Francisco with a large Chinese community, a day trip is a good place to start. Find an authentic Chinese restaurant that's representative of north or south China cuisine—quite different from one another. Here's an example: in the north wheat is the prevalent starch, while in the south, it's rice.

In the restaurant, listen to knowledgeable, English speaking servers. Take the food recommendations that fit your current tastes most closely. Become more adventuresome over time but without uneasiness. Do it at your own pace. Space your visits to match your appetite for change. Pushing yourself can backfire.

What if food isn't your issue? Perhaps you fear being trapped in a plane or on a ship. The same process applies. Say you want to take a cruise. Don't make yourself start with a ship that takes you around the rough waters surrounding Cape Horn. This venue navigates around the tip of South America passing through the rough sea where the Atlantic and Pacific Oceans meet—only a few hundred miles from Antarctica. Does this make you uneasy?

Photo 27: Nearing Cape Horn: the rough waters of the Antarctic Ocean

Maybe start by visiting a local cruise ship terminal/port. First notice the ship's size, then its construction. Find the life boats, then see if you can get an in-port tour by explaining your concerns. A second step might be to visit a permanently docked ship like the Queen Mary in Long Beach, CA. Spend a day onboard with the understanding that this is an old ship, no longer seaworthy but safely anchored. You'll come away with some useful impressions.

Watch the change process unfold. The next step? Maybe a harbor tour to see the sights of a city from the water—with land close enough to quell any jitters. Then you might branch out to a river cruise where the shoreline on both sides of the boat is always visible. And finally, here are some additional strategies from behavior focused therapy that support inwardly focused changes:

- Nurture yourself with supportive self talk. Encouragement goes a long way to soothe jitters.

- Create an exaggerated, worse case travel scenario, beyond believability—to contrast with the likely outcome. The truth is somewhere in between and usually not so bad. If the food in your chosen destination is really uneatable, a loaf of bread and a hunk of cheese, or a handful of nuts, are always an option and will ward off starvation. Protein bars are good in a pinch even for dinner.

- Reward yourself tangibly or intangibly for successive approximations toward your goal, or for a positive end result. For example, a fine desert for a foodie or concert tickets for a music lover might make the effort worthwhile.

- Celebrate if you've conquered the fear of flying, or ocean travel, or any other hurdle. You'll be one step closer to the next challenge—which will seem more manageable.

- Notice and appreciate any patterns of incremental success. That means learning to identify new ways to master your discomforts using the tools that worked before: become comfortable, for example, in forests, on mountains, crossing oceans, exploring big cities, mastering heights, or achieving any behavior that feels beyond your current reach. Keep in mind, if you've crossed the Atlantic Ocean, the next ocean won't be all that different.

Remember to take very small steps on the road toward mastery. And mastery increases the feeling of success. Success increases your confidence to take new steps. And so on.

Some Final Thoughts

The previous fifty-one mini chapters provided only a brief sampling of opportunities for experiencing life and place. Surely you can extend these as your journey meanders through time. It turns out that everything you do informs and enriches your existence.

The journey never ends until our last breath is exhaled—and beyond that, who knows. Until then, the *Inward Traveler* makes new connections between an ever evolving *inner* world, increasingly complex as we age, and the *outer* world. Also, the physical world continues to change in predictable and in less predictable ways— creating infinite possibilities for exploration and investigation.

The kaleidoscope of these dynamic forces help us form fresh patterns and move in novel directions. And so the opportunity for new reflections and observations will always be there to enhance our lives. Older only means richer, wiser. Creativity has no limitations—not age, life circumstances, gender, ethnicity, or even I.Q.

Several years ago when I retired from my life as a practicing psychologist, I thought my learning was done and the future might be simply more of the same. Little did I know then that beginning to play the cello would have a profound interaction with my travels. But that's just what happened.

No sooner do I arrive at any destination than I search for the music. Upon arriving in Prague, the Czech Republic, I was captured by string quartets playing on street corners and outside of coffee shops, giving the listener a taste of beauty with a promise of more to come later that evening in local churches. I dream about, hear, look for, and find myself amazed by any manner of music or musician.

Pan pipes sounded heavenly in a Sunday market in Ecuador. Who would have guessed? Yes, I found them there. I wasn't looking but I did stop to notice with piqued interest. My love of music led me to playing the cello in recent years. You can return to the chapter in this book called: "Awe: seeing life with a beginner's mind," to review the pan pipe details.

Photo 28: Pan pipe demonstration in Manta, Ecuador

In Wuhan, China I heard a classical Chinese orchestra playing music on ancient instruments, tuned in slightly jarring ways, and producing delightful but non-Western sounds Found by accident? Maybe. But when you start studying something, like I did music, you open new channels of interest and intention, and it leads you down previously unknown paths. If you couple that with sharpened senses and mindfulness, you've opened a new portal into a nascent adventure.

And so it goes. Take the 51 chapter themes and run with them in any direction your heart, mind, and spirit choose. I promise that the journey you'll create will be extraordinary and well worth the effort.

Quiz: Find Your Travel Style

Here are some questions to help you think and feel your way to your optimal travel experience. Select your best fitting answer for each question:

1. How do you see yourself?

❑ *energetic, active, dynamic*   *(3)*

❑ *adventurous*   *(3)*

❑ *soulful, spiritual*   *(1)*

❑ *worldly, sophisticated*   *(2)*

❑ *quiet*   *(1)*

❑ *thinking type*   *(2)*

2. How do you describe your interests?

❑ *creative, artistic*   *(1)*

❑ *sports, hard play*   *(3)*

❑ *adventurous, thrill seeking*   *(3)*

❑ *sensual, dreamy*   *(1)*

❑ *educational, health oriented*   *(2)*

❑ *historical*   *(2)*

3. What is your preferred environment?

❑ *city, urban*   *(3)*

❑ *historical*   *(2)*

❑ *nature*   *(1)*

❑ *rural, rustic*   *(1)*

❑ *spiritual*   *(1)*

❏ *calming, restful* *(1)*

❏ *exciting, invigorating* *(3)*

4. How do you use travel?
Time frame:

❏ *frequent but short trips* *(3)*

❏ *extended period: two weeks or more* *(2)*

❏ *immersion: months at a time* *(1)*

Tempo:

❏ *to invigorate, excite* *(3)*

❏ *to relax* *(1)*

❏ *to learn* *(2)*

5. How do others see you?

❏ *relaxed, laid back* *(1)*

❏ *playful, fun loving* *(3)*

❏ *worldly, sophisticated* *(2)*

❏ *mindful, reflective* *(1)*

❏ *serious* *(2)*

❏ *nature oriented* *(1)*

6. In each of the following pairs, which describes your preferred vacation style?

❏ *novel* *(3) vs. familiar* *(1)*

❏ *simple* *(1) vs. indulgent* *(3)*

❏ *slow* *(1) vs. fast paced* *(3)*

❏ *convenience (1) vs. hardship, challenging*   *(3)*

❏ *solo   (1) vs. accompanied*   *(3)*

❏ *amusement (3) vs. growth*   *(1)*

❏ *single focus (1) vs. multi-focal: "Tuesday, it must be Belgium!" (3)*

Quiz scoring:

This quiz has no right or wrong answers because travel style, personal history, and personality affect choices in unique ways. Over time you might respond to these questions differently.

For today, reflect on your answers, then add your scores which will range from 5-15. Question #6 guides your choice of a physical setting. Score it separately by selecting one from each pair and adding the score associated with it from 7-21.

The Inward Traveler will help you identify venues that are keyed to your styles and preferences.

Understanding your scores:

Scores of 12-15 suggest: adventure, love of novelty, excitement, fast-paced, challenge, play, ultra -sports;

Scores of 9-12 suggest: orientation toward history, learning, serious, and growth-oriented activities which may be compatible with tours;

Scores of 5-8 suggest: quiet, soulful, spiritual, and mindful. You might be seeking creative, calming, relaxing venues, and valuing alone-time;

Question 6 scoring:

If your score is:
7-10 it suggests: a slower, easier and less stressful pace;
16-21 it suggests: a more complex and hurried pace;
11-15 it suggests: greatest flexibility and compatibility with co-travelers, making it easier to choose a venue.

Alternate scoring:

You may find that you've checked two or more boxes in any one or more of the quiz categories. In that case, you can complete a separate quiz for each set of responses. After all, we are not always binary—either one way or another. Forcing ourselves into little boxes is not the goal of this book!

Acknowledgments:

I am grateful to the world around me for providing so many awesome reminders of beauty and meaning. I appreciate the encouragement of everyone whose lives touched mine in this journey, stimulating my creativity, while supporting and clarifying my thoughts, ideas, and passions.

More specifically, I appreciate the very concrete and helpful comments from friends and former students who were willing to be candid as well as kind in their feedback. My "book club" buddies, Judy Passanante, June Loy and Nancy Hogan were the first to read the whole unedited manuscript and take a stab at making it a far better read.

My "beta readers," Sally Karlin, Paul Klunder, Diane Means, and David Ohst provided priceless perceptions from their own perspectives, greatly enriching the project. Although editing wasn't something they signed up for, they all seemed to find inelegant wordings and missing commas.

Thanks especially to Virginia Kidd, Ph.D., my long time academic colleague, friend, and sister in writing, who listened painstakingly to my ongoing stream of grumbles about this project, witnessed my struggle with the writing process, and supported my efforts for many years.

And finally, my deepest appreciation goes to my best friend, husband, and skilled writer, Joe Hustein. He was willing to go to battle with me over a phrase or a chapter that he felt could be better communicated. He sometimes knew how to say what I meant even when I couldn't articulate it. He deserves a medal for putting up with me!

Appendix: Places mentioned

Page 15   Manta, Ecuador
Page 18   Cape Horn, Chile and Ushuaia, Argentina
Page 25   Atlantic Ocean and Mediterranean Sea meet
Page 30   Northern California
Page 33   Bodega Bay, California
Page 37   Kauai, Hawaii
Page 49   Edinburgh, Scotland
Page 51   The Cloisters Museum, New York City
Page 53   Norwegian fjords
Page 55   Kyoto, Japan
Page 66   Shell Beach, California
Page 71   Miltenberg, Germany
Page 72   Istanbul, Turkey
Page 75   Waimea Canyon, Kauai, Hawaii
Page 78   Shimizu, Japan
Page 87   Hong Kong
Page 98   Guilin, China
Page 108   Istanbul, Turkey
Page 114   Hanalei Bay, Kauai, Hawaii
Page 118   Chilean fjords, Chile, South America
Page 133   Patagónico Sur, South America
Page 141   Buenos Aires, Argentina
Page 154   Kauai and Honolulu, Hawaii
Page 158   Panama Canal, Panama
Page 178   Hong Kong
Page 198   Manta, Ecuador

What others said about Toder's last book: *The Vintage Years*

"…Toder's scientific acumen and the inspiration of these exceptional—yet everyday—elders will be sure to kick-start readers' explorations of their own late-in-the-game creative potential."
—*Publishers' Weekly*

"*The Vintage Years* provides us with a vision of the future and ways to get there that are positive, practical, and make the future something to look forward to."
— Louis Cozolino, Ph.D. Professor of Psychology, Pepperdine University and author of *The Healthy Aging Brain*

"*The Vintage Years* is a must for anyone who has always dreamed of unleashing their creativity but has put it off their whole lives, much recommended."
—*The Midwest Book Review*

"…inspirational and comprehensive…. *The Vintage Years* confirms my strong belief that it is never to late to learn and engage in arts and that by doing so we create a healthier, joyful, positive, more fulfilling life…."
— Biana Kovic, Cellist, Filmmaker (*Virtuoso: It's Never Too Late to Learn*)

"It is the best motivational book for elders that I've so far encountered."
—*San Francisco Book Review*

Photo 29: Author, writing leisurely aboard a ship in the Pacific Ocean

About the Author

Francine Toder, Ph.D. is an emeritus faculty member of California State University, Sacramento and is a clinical psychologist retired from private practice. She is also the author of *When Your Child Is Gone: Learning to Live Again, Your Kids Are Grown: Moving On With and Without Them, and The Vintage Years: Finding your Inner Artist (Writer, Musician, Visual Artist) After Sixty*. Her extensive writing on diverse topics appears in magazines, professional journals, newspapers, blog sites such as *Huffington Post, Next Avenue* and *Thrive Global*, as well as edited book chapters. She resides with her husband in the San Francisco Bay Area.